PAINT TO WIN

Creative Strategic Management

Ronald M. Lowy

University Press of America,® Inc.
Dallas · Lanham · Boulder · New York · Oxford

Copyright © 2003 by
University Press of America,® Inc.
4501 Forbes Boulevard
Suite 200
Lanham, Maryland 20706
UPA Acquisitions Department (301) 459-3366

PO Box 317
Oxford
OX2 9RU, UK

Library of Congress Control Number: 2003114124
ISBN 0-7618-2703-X (clothbound : alk. ppr.)

This book is dedicated to
my mom and dad.

Contents

Acknowledgements

I would like to acknowledge the following:
My students who have listened and provided input, Glen Nelson who
helped me with the editing and formatting, and John Hebert who helped
with the chapter on implementation.

Introduction

Most successful people are driven by the desire to reach their full potential. This is especially true in business where the stakes are so high. It doesn't matter if you are someone wanting to start a business, someone who is running their own business or if you are the chief executive of a major corporation, your personal goal is to make your organization stand out from all others.

Since there are so many of you, there are plenty of people who are willing to show you how to be successful. Their approaches differ in style, but they are all the same in that they offer specific solutions for specific problems. For example, how to expand, contract, take a niche approach, etc... However, something must be wrong because many large and small businesses using these generic approaches are failing. Why aren't these well publicized and widely taught approaches working? The answer is that no two managers, workforces, businesses, problems or situations are the same. So, it doesn't take a genius to discover that pat generic solutions are not going to do it. Any attempt to provide an all-inclusive approach to lead a company to success must show a way to develop creative and unique solutions to the vast array of differing problems. The trouble is, to date, creativity has been left out of the equation.

This book will help those interested in owning and operating successful businesses. It will provide a new approach for students and business people to gain an understanding of the intra-relationships between the many functional areas of a business and its inter-relationship to the surrounding environment. This nontraditional approach is different in that it provides you with the tools necessary to allow you too fully utilize your own creativity. It does not simply focus on providing a limited list of available strategies. This text, and the approach described, goes much further. It requires you to think and be creative in order to develop unique, successful strategies. For those of you who have business experience, have taken business courses, or read other business books, this book is designed to further enhance your current understanding of business. For those of you with no background in business, this book will help you develop an understanding of how to successfully manage a business.

The one goal of any business leader or entrepreneur is to create workable strategic options and problem solutions that lead to success. As previously stated, creative actions, along with an understanding of how to properly use the tools of business are necessary to develop successful strategic options. Yet, it is important to note that there is nothing this book, or any other book, can give you that will be a guaranteed step-by-step, automatic formula for success. It just doesn't work that way. If that were possible someone would have already written that book, everyone would have read it, and we would all be vastly successful. We cannot all be so fortunate, however, because for every leader there have to be some followers. There are no magic bullets for success.

The problem is that in addition to having the ability and the understanding of how to create unique solutions and strategies, you sometimes need a little luck. This means that the best business approaches can only increase the probability of success. For example, when I used to play Monopoly, I won more than I lost when I held the moderately priced orange properties. Other players would try to stock up on the Railroads, or Boardwalk and Park Place. Anyone who has played the game knows that these properties accrue a lot of money. But that is not the way to win. A computer study, which surveyed thousands of Monopoly games, found that the players who held the orange properties were the ones that won more often than with any other combination. This does not mean that you will not win if you do not obtain the orange properties. You could still win with a little luck, but, by acquiring the orange properties, you are only increasing the probability of winning. Just like in the game of Monopoly, in the world of business there is some luck involved. If you take the wrong approach there is a possibility, though very slim, that you will win.

Taking the wrong approach in business has lead to some success stories. But, the probability is that you will lose. Considering the amount (approximately 85%) of business failures, it never hurts to play the odds.

Contrary to conventional wisdom, business is an art, not a science and a successful business should be thought of as a work of art. A person in business uses tools that can be considered "scientific," but developing and operating a successful business is an art form. I often equate it to, and this book will use, the concepts of painting. I will instruct you, much like an art teacher would show you the correct brush to use, how to mix colors, and provide you with specific techniques that can help you paint beautifully; but you must do the painting.

It is useful to understand that in business, as in art, there are three categories of manager-artists. The first category is made up of those who know nothing at all about the art of business. They think it looks easy and believe it's something they should try. This category is represented by thousands of entrepreneurs who do not take the time to develop an understanding of the art of business. These are the "amateurs". The probability of their success is very low.

The second category of managers includes the business mechanics. They have learned a certain set of procedures and they diligently follow them. They copy what others have done and do what they are told. However, managers in this category can never be better than the current leader. Unfortunately many of our current business managers fall into this category.

Managers in the third category are the artists. They know what the tools are and how to use them to manage a prosperous organization. These people are formed at the core of all successful businesses. They utilize sound proven business practices and develop new creative solutions and strategies. By reading and understanding this book, you too can become a business artist and lead your company to the winner's circle.

The principles and techniques developed in this book can be used in all types of organizations, whether small, medium sized, or large. They can also be used in sub-groups of an organization such as a division or team. They can be for-profit organizations or not-for-profit. They could be service companies, such as law firms, or manufacturing conglomerates. In order to facilitate our discussion, when providing an example I will use a different terminology for differing organizational types.

When using a small company as an example, I will talk about one with a single product or service. I will use the terminology "product or service lines" when the examples are for a medium-sized company. Since large companies often break into units, when an example incorporates a large organization, I will refer to the organization's "strategic business units" (SBU's).

A Strategic Business Unit (SBU) is a grouping of products, product lines or business units linked together for some synergetic reason. "Synergy" occurs when the combined parts of something are greater than the sum of the individual parts. Simply put, synergy is one plus one equals three.

For example, let's suppose those two organizations or groups within one organization are to be combined. One organization has a great production department but a poor marketing department that often fails to sell all it produces. The other has a great marketing department but a poor production group. Sales are often delayed since it is unable to produce the required amounts. Each of these organizations generates revenues of $75,000. After production and marketing costs of $25,000, each earns a profit of $50,000. Together, yet operating on their own, they have combined revenues of $150,000, costs of $50,000, and profits of $100,000. If the organization were to combine these two into one unit, it could eliminate one bad marketing group and one bad production group. This would result in half the total costs. Even if it still only generated the same revenue, with the reduced cost, its combined profits would be $125,000. This is synergy.

Before I continue, there are some other basic definitions that also must be discussed. The first is strategic management. This text is designed to talk about business strategies and strategic problem solutions. By "strategic," I mean strategies and solutions that are developed to assure the long term viability of the organization. Long term generally means five years, although it differs for each business and industry. Five years may be too long for a computer business, but for an energy business five years may be too short. Keep in mind that what you do for your business will affect you short term as well as long-term. However, when you address strategic management, generally you should plan for long-term solutions.

It's important to note that strategy is constantly changing. Even if a five-year plan is developed, a company must constantly monitor and adjust its strategy depending on what is happening in the environment around it.

A policy is a set of procedures that is put into place to help achieve the objectives of the strategic plan. For example, Company A's policy is to promote from within rather than hiring outside the company. The object of this policy is to help achieve a better, more competitive work force.

To make it easier for you, I have formatted this book in the following manner. First, you must lay out your palette. This is covered in Chapter 1 where the Strategic Options Outline is explained. Once your palette is laid out, your canvas must be primed and the outline defining what you will paint must be put into place. This is explained in Chapter 2: Getting Started: The Strategic Planning Process. The remaining chapters, 3 through 8, discuss the basic methods that provide each painter with the ability to choose the right designs and colors for a successful strategy.

I have included examples to illustrate the issue being discussed, which I was a little reluctant to include because many of them illustrate specific solutions to unique problems occurring in a particular company. But, as I said before, this is not a book about specific answers. It is a book about ways to develop innovative solutions, so remember that the examples are only illustrations.

Now, let's do some painting.

Chapter 1

The Strategic Palette

Strategic Options Outline

In order to successfully create a masterpiece, the first step that a master artist takes is to place on his or her palette all of the available colors that may be required to paint the picture. The layout is done in a very purposeful manner, allowing the painter to easily select and combine different colors. A palette that is laid out correctly and completely adds to the painter's ability to be creative. An incomplete palette constrains the painter's ability to put down on the canvas what he or she desires. The same is true when creating successful strategies.

The strategic options palette is like the painter's palette. It facilitates the generation of any possible strategic approach that can lead to a prosperous successful business. This Strategic Options Palette (Figure 1.1) does not list every possible strategy. Instead it provides the creative planner with the elements necessary to develop creative successful strategies. It is the source of all strategies. All the materials on it are pragmatic and practical, and this strategic options palette can be used for any type or size of business.

This "painting" approach is unique, but it is very practical and you will not have to memorize it. It should be just common sense. This is the tool that you will use to guide your company, whether it is a small entrepreneurial company, a division or a large corporation.

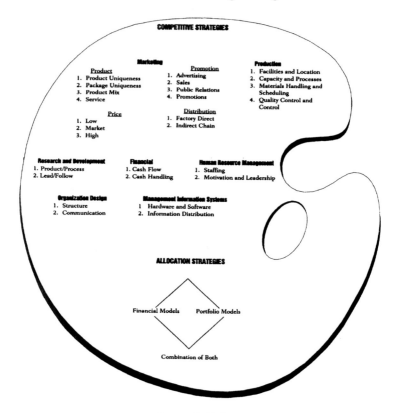

Strategic Pallet
Figure 1.1

Strategy Types And Levels

Besides the lack of creativity, one of the problems that has hindered the development of useful strategy development is the confusion about types and levels of strategies. Differing authors will discuss a large assortment of types and levels of strategies that are often divergent and confusing. For example, one business textbook alludes to numerous types of business strategies, including whimsical groupings such as underdog and low market share business strategies, dominant firm strategies, growth market strategies, weak businesses strategies, mature or declining industry strategies, and turnaround strategies.

Simply listing types of strategies does not facilitate the selection of an appropriate strategy. Since each of these strategies is prescribed for a specific circumstance, one could conclude that a strategy that may work for a business with low market share may not be appropriate for a business in an emerging industry. This is far from reality.

Other authors discuss levels of strategy. They believe that strategies differ at various levels of the organization, such as the corporate, line, functional, and operating level. All of this simply adds to the confusion, restricts creativity and generally makes it more difficult for someone trying to succeed.

In this book, you will not learn specific strategies and strategy types. You will learn the tools that will help you form your own strategy or solve an organizational problem using the Strategic Options Outline/Palette.

This common sense creative approach to strategy formulation and selection dictates that strategies can be grouped into two basic categories: Allocation Strategies and Competitive Strategies. These two strategic groupings can be conducted at any level in the organization. All strategies fall within these two types. This is the only categorization that you need to understand to develop that creative approach which will ensure the long-term viability of your organization. Remember that the process is only a tool, you must create the strategy yourself.

Allocation Strategies

Allocation strategies are strategies that help an organization optimally distribute its resources. It is important to understand that resources include not only financial resources, but human resources and physical resources as well. Human resources are all of the members of both the work force and management. Physical resources consist of plant, property and equipment. Financial resources include all the funds available to the business, including cash on hand and cash available through credit.

Allocation strategies are often called corporate strategies because managers at "corporate headquarters" are often the ones responsible for the proper handling of the organization's resources But, resource allocation does in fact take place at all levels of the organization.

The probability of allocating resources in an effective manner can be increased significantly through the use of three models. These include Financial Models, Portfolio Models and a combination of both.

Financial Models

Financial models are problem-solving tools that enable the business manager or owner to make resource allocation decisions by using basic financial information. Financial models can be grouped into two types depending upon their complexity. The simplest type involves the use of raw financial data and ratio analysis. An example of using raw financial data would be the decision to go with a business unit that generates more cash than another business unit. An example using financial ratio analysis would include using a ratio such as return-on-investment (ROI) to compare organizational units. For example, if you had two business units and one returned 19% and the other returned 14%, you would invest more of your resources in the first unit with the higher ROI.

A more complex approach to resource allocation utilizes financial models involving the use of multiple financial ratios and the consideration of other information that directly affects the value of the financial resource. This group typically includes the consideration of the level of risk that accompanies the expected return. A well-known financial model in this group is the Capital Asset Pricing Model, where there is a given value of risk that accompanies each investment.

Let's say, for example, that you wanted to allocate resources between two units within your organization or between two products that you chose to make. Even though one returned 20% and the other returned 15%, you might elect to go with the 15% return if it was guaranteed and the other was not.

Other types of complex financial models consider varying types of financial data, including diverse bits of information such as stock market performance. It seems that the approaches are limited only to the number of consulting firms and college professors that have developed their own financial models.

As with most things in life, there are pros and cons to the choices we make. The same is true when choosing ways to allocate resources. Financial models were very popular a few years ago. Perhaps this was due to their simplicity, availability of the data and the fact that the data are quantifiable and easily comparable. However, what one really should be concerned with are the cons. It is good to keep in mind that the pros help you, but the cons can destroy you. You must be aware of the negative unintended consequences of the choices you make. Be careful.

The major drawback of financial models is that they do not consider the interrelationships between different organizational investments. In other words, they do not consider the synergistic relationship between your company's products, product lines, or strategic business units. The best way to illustrate this is through the following example. Imagine that your company is made up of three strategic business units (SBUs). These are their returns:

SBU #1 20% Return on investment (ROI)
SBU #2 10% Return on investment (ROI)
SBU #3 5% Return on investment (ROI)

Using only financial models, it could be argued that you should focus most of your company's resources on SBU #1 since it's ROI is twice that of any other SBU. In addition, you might also want to allocate some resources to SBU #2 and even less to SBU #3. However, assume that SBU #1 produces bolts, SBU #2 produces nails and SBU #3 produces machine nuts. If you follow the financial model, its possible that you could seriously jeopardize your company's chance for success since it would be difficult to maintain sales in your bolt division (SBU #1) if you did not continue to support the nut division (SBU #3). It is not unusual for companies to frequently have interrelationships between their strategic business units. You will learn more about financial models in Chapter 4.

Portfolio Models

Portfolio modeling is the second basic approach to allocating resources. Portfolio models make up for the deficiencies of financial models in that they consider synergistic relationships. They look at the entire organization as a whole. They do this by comparing each product, product line or SBU using some measure to evaluate the worth of the market place or industry, and some measure of the company's ability to compete in that industry. In other words, they ask of each product, product line, or SBU two questions. The first asks if this is a good business for our company to be in, and the second asks if the company has what it takes to be successful. Generally, competitiveness is measured on the horizontal axis and the worth of the industry is measured on the vertical axis. These two factors are then cross-classified in a matrix format, which is called a portfolio model

(Figure 1.2). Accordingly, you would be willing to commit a significant amount of your resources to a business unit that was in a very good industry, such as one with high growth, and one that took advantage of your strong organizational attributes. One the other hand, you would not invest in a business unit that was in a poorly performing industry such as one with declining growth and, in addition, did not have the necessary skills to be competitive.

Like financial models, portfolio models have positive and negative aspects. As mentioned above, the positive aspect is that they take into consideration the synergistic relationship among all of the elements of the business. The negative aspect is that portfolio models are often subjective and therefore, their users can arbitrarily modify their results.

I
n
d
u
s
t
r
y

O
u
t
l
o
o
k

Our Competitiveness In This Industry

Figure 1.2

There are many different portfolio models. This is because each author has recognized the negative subjectivity of portfolio models. Each author has then tried to develop his or her own model, which lessens the impact of the user's subjectivity. There are well-known and well-used portfolio models. One is the Four Cell Market Growth Rate/Relative Market Share Model, initially developed by the Boston Consulting Group. The other is the Nine-Cell Industry Attractiveness/Business Strength Model, originally developed by

McKinsey and General Electric. You will learn more about these in Chapter 6: Painting Techniques.

Combining Models

When you are not sure of which model to use, you can use both. In fact, you can choose several financial models and several portfolio models. Using more than one is actually beneficial for your analysis. The more information you acquire, the more accurate you will be. This is especially applicable in business, since information can often be inaccurate and hard to obtain. If business information is in fact inaccurate and not readily available, what is the value of it? The answer and explanation lies in the use of combinations of different models as illustrated in a Venn Diagram.

A Venn Diagram is an illustration of overlapping circles (Figure 1.3). Each of the circles has an area that is unique to itself and another area that overlaps the other circles. For our discussion, each circle represents the information obtained through the use of a

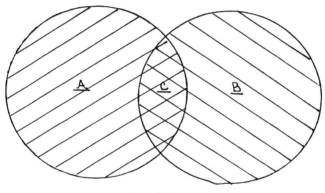

Venn Diagram
Figure 1.3

particular model. The area of a circle A represents the set of data derived from one model. The area of circle B represents a set of data derived from another model. The area C represents the data from circle A and circle B that is in agreement. So you can see that each approach has some mutually agreeable information. It is this mutually agreeable information derived from the use of differing approaches that provides you with some degree of certainty.

The use of only one model will give you *some* information, but you will not know how accurate it is. If you check that information using another model and in some areas get the same results, you increase the probability of making the right decisions. If you use a third model and again find overlapping information, the probability that you are correct is even greater. The more models you use, the greater the probability of having valid information, which can aid you in making the right decisions.

In summary, there are three basic approaches that you can use to determine, or help you determine, how to optimally allocate your resources. The first are financial models, which are based on financial data. The second are portfolio models, which use some measure of the market and some measure of your company's ability to compete. Third are combination approaches, which use both financial and portfolio models. It is to your advantage to use the combination approach when possible, utilizing as many financial and portfolio models that time and money will allow. For instance, if portfolio model analyses indicate that SBU's A and B are good investments and SBU C is not so good, and at the same time financial models indicate that SBUs A and B are good investments and that SBU C is not so good, then this agreement is a reliable indication of a successful approach to resource allocation.

Competitive Strategies

In order to create a successful strategy, and develop solutions to your organization problems, it's not enough to simply allocate your resources in an optimal manner. Your organization must do something different and better than the competition, something that allows you to stand out from the others and hold an advantage in the marketplace. Competitive strategies are the group of creative moves that allow you to secure that advantage and are developed from within the organization.

The problem with developing successful competitive strategies is not that they are so difficult to develop, it is that they can come from anywhere within the organization. So, you need to do what every good painter does: arrange this side of your "palette" in a manner that allows for easy selection. This can best be done by taking the logical approach and dividing the organization into its six functional areas and one additional area that encompasses the organization as a whole.

These areas consist of:

1. Marketing
2. Production
3. Research & Development
4. Management Information Systems
5. Human Resource Management
6. Finance
7. Organizational Design

What you are about to learn is the pragmatic applicability of everything you have discovered through experience on the job, in previous business classes, and from other books you may have read. Only this time you will have a palette of strategic options laid out in front of you, which will help you use your knowledge of business and even the things you may have forgotten. Let's see how this all fits together so you can truly understand the logic of it all - not just memorize it, but really know it. The first area on the "competitive" side of the strategic palette is marketing.

Marketing

1) PRODUCT
   a) product
   b) package
   c) mix
   d) service

2) PRICE
   a) high
   b) market
   c) low

3) PROMOTION
    a) promotions
    b) public relations
    c) personal selling
    d) advertising

4) DISTRIBUTION
    a) direct
    b) indirect

When the subject of competitive strategy is discussed, the first thing most people think of is marketing. Organizations generally rely on their sales force and advertisers to help them achieve a competitive position in the marketplace. However, marketing is much more than that. Marketing involves developing a product or a group of products or services that meets a potential customer's needs. In addition, marketing considers how best to inform the consumer about the product, establish the appropriate price for the product, and assure that the product is readily available. Most often, marketing strategies are divided into what is known as the "marketing mix", also known as Jerome McCarthy's "4 P's of Marketing: Product, Price, Promotion and Place." By using this concept, the Marketing section of your palette should be arranged to include:

- Product Strategies
- Pricing Strategies
- Promotion Strategies
- Place (distribution) Strategies

Product Strategies

There are many types of product strategies. In fact, there are so many that your palette needs to be divided into even smaller sections. To this end, the product strategy area of the strategic options palette is segmented into four distinct areas. They include: product, package, service, and mix.

Product

There are many successful product strategies. A product can be made bigger, faster, smoother, better, tougher, new and improved, etc. Today, one of the most popular ways companies making food products are changing their product is by making it fat free or "lighter", with fewer calories. Can you think of any? Remember though, when changing your product, you must try to provide better value or a better way to meet your customer's needs.

Don't be confused by the Product Strategy example I just gave. Your company's product does not have to be something you can touch. It can be a service you provide. If you are a consultant, your product is the knowledge you provide to your clients. If you belong to a law firm, it is your legal advice. How can I modify my "service" product? If for example, I tutor students, I may utilize the internet to provide better learning examples. What about other "service" products? The answer is up to you and your creative abilities. As I say, "paint!"

Package

A company can also improve the product by changing the product's package. One example is to change the cap on a bottle of laundry detergent to serve as a measuring cup that has a dripless spout. Another example is to package the product in a square box instead of a round bottle. This would make it easier for the distributor to stock, providing the distributor with a reason to buy that product over another product. Other examples of using packaging to achieve a competitive advantage would be to change the color of the package or the picture on the box, allowing the product stand out on the store shelf. Today the environment is important to consumers. They want their products packaged in environmentally safe containers. I'll bet you can think of many ways to change the package, making it more appealing to the customer.

Service

Some products have to be the same and/or come in similar packages, like mechanic's tools or Ford pick-up trucks. So why do you go to Sears to by tools, and why do you pick one Ford dealer over another? Could it be the service that is provided with the product? Sears is known for service, a factor consumers consider when choosing where to by their tools. There is a well-known auto dealer who every Sunday invites his customers in for a barbecue. He then provides lectures and instructions on how to operate and maintain their new cars. You can bet he has an advantage over the competition.

Mix

The last component under Product is the mix of products. Mix of products means that often a combination of products is strategically better than just one product. For example, a company that produces bolts should probably make nuts and washers as well. We often shop at department stores vs. specialty stores because we can get several items with just one visit. Another example of the strategic mix approach would be to have a group of products that can be produced or distributed synergistically. An example of this is the product mix of BIC shavers and BIC lighters. There may seem to be no connection, but in fact there is. Both of these are sold by using point-of-sale displays. The synergy lies in the efficiency of allowing the distribution of both at the same time by just one person.

When discussing marketing and success in business, think first of how something unique can be done in the Product area. Ask yourself: What can be done with the product? What can be done with the package? What can be done with the mix? What can be done with the service? Much has been written about these questions. When making a decision, look at what others have done, but also learn to create your own unique approaches. Go to the Product area of your palette and "paint!"

Pricing Strategies

Your options to achieve an advantage over the competition using pricing are simple. There are only three approaches a company can take. They include low, high, and market.

Low

The obvious and most often considered approach is low price. Lowering the product's price will attract the consumer, but beware of this approach. This is a very dangerous strategy. Very few companies can win with just a low pricing strategy. For this to be a successful strategy, you need to be either very efficient or have a lot of money. Entire industries have been decimated by price wars. The airline industry is a good example of this. Since this is such an important issue, more on this will be discussed later.

High

The second and often overlooked pricing strategy is high pricing. It is often hard to convince organizations of this, but it has merit.

Toothpaste is an example of competitive high pricing. Have you ever compared the prices of generic toothpaste to brand name toothpaste? Some stores have sold generic baking soda, fluoride toothpaste for $.49 for four ounces and Aqua-fresh toothpaste with exactly the same ingredients for $2.59. Did you think to yourself that the tube for .49 cents can't be as good as the one for $2.59? So, you bought the one for $2.59. You are not alone. Why do many consumers reject generic products even though they are basically the same products? The answer is that consumers usually associate better quality with the higher priced, brand name products.

There are numerous cases of successful companies choosing the high price strategy and unsuccessful companies who chose to price low. When producing a luxury product, a customer assumes that there is a high price attached to it. If a company produces a luxury product and charges too little, the consumer may not buy it because they may think it is really not a "luxury" item, so the prestige of owning a high priced item will be lost. It has been argued that the demise of the DeLorean, a low-priced, high-prestige sports car was caused by this.

Market

The third pricing strategy is choosing the market price. This choice generally eliminates price as a competitive factor. Market pricing doesn't "rock-the-boat" and allows other strategies to become more effective.

Promotion Strategies

Promotion is the third element of the marketing mix. Like product strategies, there are many ways to be competitive in the area of Promotion. Promotional strategies can be broken down to three P's and an A: promotions, public relations, personal selling, and advertising.

Promotions

The first area under the Promotion element is promotions, which typically includes giveaways or sweepstakes. Ed McMahon has probably sold more magazine subscriptions than anyone else by using this technique.   Remember the "You just won the million dollar sweepstakes" campaign? There are, literally, thousands of winning strategies, which can be developed under the promotion area of your strategic palette. Cigarette companies are known for their promotions. They give away millions of free cigarettes, hoping that they can hook you on their brand. When using this technique, the important thing to remember is to be creative.

Public Relations

Public relations is the often "free" communication between your company and its customers. Company sales can be increased, or a disaster avoided with affective public relations. A company that got its big start through the effective use of public relations was Ben and Jerry's Homemade Inc.

Ben and Jerry's Homemade Inc. used its concern for the environment to improve customer relations. When the environment was becoming a strong issue, Ben and Jerry's office manager, Gail Mayville, received the Business Enterprise Environment Award for her research of business and its environment. Her research showed that the top three items in need of recycling were cardboard, paper and plastics. She subsequently launched Ben and Jerry's into a well publicized recycling program with the following press release: "... [our] goal is to be 100% involved in responsibly managing our solid waste stream, conserving energy sources and developing environmentally beneficial community outreach programs."   This is a company that actively communicated a positive company image to the public by publicizing its concern for the environment.   Many consumers chose Ben and Jerry's ice cream because of this.

Personal Selling

The most successful companies are very often, the companies utilizing strategies that allow them to have the most efficient and affective sales force. There are literally hundreds of books written about sales force management.

Today there exists a very successful company that almost went bankrupt because its sales program was based on a poorly devised sales motivation scheme.   The sales team was encouraged to sell to the company's independent distributors. It did such a good job that the distributors were buying product even though the company was not moving it. As a result, the company's sales forecast was inaccurate and the distributors were all on the verge of going out of business.

In response, the company made one small change. Instead of basing the sales force's incentive pay on what they sold, the company based it on what its distributors sold. The distributors were ecstatic since the company's sales force was helping them sell to their customers. Now the company was much more successful since it knew the level of inventory held by the distributors and was able to schedule production in a much more efficient manner. In addition, not only had they saved their valuable distribution network, but overall sales increased. This is just one of many possibilities of creative "painting" that can have its origins from the personal selling area of the strategic palette.

Advertising

The last area on your strategic palette under promotion is advertising. Advertising agencies have made millions of dollars for themselves and the companies they represent by creating ad campaigns that help their companies gain the competitive edge. One noted example is; "Just for the Taste of It...Diet Coke." Coke could have introduced their diet soft drink as a diet product, but they understood the sensitivity of people who are overweight. So instead of saying, drink Diet Coke, and you will stay or become slim, they said, drink Diet Coke, "Just for the Taste of It." You too can think of creative approaches to advertising.

Distribution Strategies

The last element of the marketing mix is Distribution. There are only two kinds of distribution, or actually two ends of a continuum of distribution strategies. At one end is direct distribution (from the factory to the customer) and at the other end is the use of a long chain of middlemen between the factory and the final user, making up the overall supply chain.

To achieve competitive success through the use of this area of your strategic palette, one must either distribute more efficiently or take the non-traditional approach. Typically, products that are very large or custom made are sold directly from the factory, while items that are generic are sold through a variety of middlemen. The non-traditional approach is exemplified in the clothing industry. Clothing that has typically been sold through a long chain of middlemen is now being sold direct from factory outlets or through catalog sales, such as L L Bean. Another example of a winning strategy that involves decreasing the distribution chain is Mary Kay Cosmetics. They created a winning distribution strategy when they initiated their door-to-door approach. They were the first to break the traditional store outlet approach, and this made them very successful.

The Distribution area of the strategic palette is one area that has been tremendously impacted by the development of electronic business processes. New creative strategies are occurring almost daily, as the internet brings the buyer and seller closer together.

In summary, it should be obvious that creative marketing strategies can lead to success. However, the difficulty lies in the many possibilities that exist. Not only can you achieve success by developing unique products, competitive prices, creative promotions, and innovative distribution, but also by recognizing that within each of these areas lies a litany of possibilities and combinations. The successful companies do not simply copy or clone, they create through the use of the strategic options palette. But wait, we have just begun. There are still six other areas yet to be defined as part of your special palette.

Production

1) FACILITIES & LOCATION
2) CAPACITY & PROCESSES
3) MATERIALS HANDLING AND SCHEDULING
4) QUALITY CONTROL AND CONTROL

Production is the second area of your strategic options palette. Lately this area has received much attention. For ease of organization, production can be divided into four options on your palette. These options can be easily remembered by looking at the largest first and then getting more and more focused. The primary options to consider are the facilities that house the company's operations and location of these facilities. Within these facilities one is concerned about the second option: capacity and processes. Capacity and processes are affected by the third option: materials handling and scheduling. These are in turn are affected by the fourth option which is quality control and control.

Facilities and Location

You can often be more competitive by modernizing your facilities, allowing them to more effectively support the organization's operations. For example, improving your lighting or locating all of your facilities on one floor can increase work force efficiency.

In today's global environment, where you locate the facility itself is another very important consideration. As transportation costs soar, consideration must be given to a firm's manufacturing facilities, relationship to raw materials, labor supply, and consumers. In retailing, it is said that the three most important factors leading to success are location, location, and location.

Capacity and Processes

Within the facility are the processes used to either develop services or manufacture products. From heavy manufacturing to restaurants, the process itself can be defined as the action that adds value to the raw materials. This is just as true for service businesses. For example, it is the processes that go on in the lawyers' office - information gathering, comparing and assembling - that allow them to use their knowledge in a productive manner.

Typically, there are four types of processes: small batch, large batch or mass production, continuous, and what is often referred to as flexible manufacturing systems.

With small batch processing, singular or small numbers of units are attended to individually. Groups of people completely fill one order at a time. Typically, small batch processing is most often used with large custom-made products. It is also the popular choice in most service organizations.

With large batch or mass production methods, the processes used are broken down into small jobs. No one person handles a single unit from start to finish. Each adds his or her work at different stations along the production line. Large batch or mass production methods are typically used when producing large amounts of similar products.

With continuous production systems, the materials flow through the process without ever stopping. Continuous processing is most often used in the oil and pharmaceutical industries where raw materials are inserted into one end of the system and finished goods flow from the other end.

Flexible manufacturing systems are computer driven systems that allow for the production of any number of units. Flexible manufacturing systems are used in companies requiring the ability to respond to the individual needs of its customers, whether the demand is large or small. Not all companies have adopted this approach since it is very expensive and it may not be needed. Successful e-business techniques have fostered the growth of flexible manufacturing systems.

There are many ways to be a successful competitor using these different processes. One way is to operate your processes in a more effective and efficient manner. Another option involves creating a new process, using techniques adopted from other industries or using a process that is not typical for your industry. For example, where a company's product or service typically utilizes small batch production, it may find a way to switch to mass production. This can be illustrated in the high-tech computing industry. Originally, calculators were produced using the small batch process. This accounted for their initial high price and limited supply. As soon as the production method was switched to large batch/mass production, costs came down. It then became possible for the initiator of the process change to lower the price. The same thing occurred with computers. At one time, IBM produced personal computers one at a time. As a result, they were not very cost competitive. Now, their computers are produced on a re-engineered production line at their Florida plant. Without this change it would have been much more difficult for them to compete. Contrary to these examples, I am sure that some companies will creatively switch from mass production back to small batch. The successful approach is the one that allows the most creative company to better meet the needs of its customers.

Adjusting capacity can also allow you to be more competitive. Obviously, you need to have enough capacity to meet consumer demand, but not so much that you have to inventory lots of finished goods. Companies have also become successful by considering the concepts of economies of scale and diseconomies of scale.

Economies of scale occur when you produce more and more goods utilizing constant fixed costs. For example, a company pays $1,000 a month for rent for a building wherein they produce 1,000 units of product per month. Therefore, $1.00 of the cost for that unit comes from rent. If that same company were able to produce 2,000 units per month, then only $.50 of the cost of each unit would be rent costs. In addition, the more they make, the more efficient they become, which further lowers costs. So companies which produce more goods often have a competitive advantage.

On the other hand, if a company becomes too big in its attempt to incorporate economies of scale, diseconomies of scale can occur, making the company less competitive. Diseconomies of scale have become more relevant because of shortened product and process life cycles. In other words, because of the rapid change of technology, products that are used today may not be used ten years from now. The same is true for the equipment that makes the products.

A classic case of diseconomies of scale that left companies in a less competitive position occurred in the steel industry over the past several decades. Thinking economies of scale, the big integrated steel producers, such as U.S. Steel, used large expensive pieces of equipment to mass produce large quantities of steel. For example, they would purchase a piece of steel making machinery for $100,000,000. The time allowed to depreciate this equipment was ten years, making their yearly cost $10,000,000. If this piece of machinery could produce 10,000,000 tons of steel per year the machinery cost per ton was $1.00. However, because of the change of technology in steel production, five years after the purchase, these companies discovered that a new machine was available that could produce the same tonnage many times faster and with just half the labor. However, the large producers could not take advantage of this new technology because they had invested $100,000,000 into the machine currently being used. If they changed equipment after only five years instead of ten years, each ton of steel would have machinery costs of $2.00 instead of $1.00. This meant that they would be losing money or making very little profit, instead of making the profits they predicted when acquiring the equipment. Many similar large producers have found themselves locked into a position that did not allow them to take advantage of developing technology. As a result, many of the smaller so-called "mini-mills" became significant competitive factors in the industry. So the strategy of positive economies of scale led to the negative diseconomies of scale in a dynamic environment and resulted in a loss of competitiveness. This is the reason many companies are incorporating smaller, more flexible business units.

Materials Handling and Scheduling

Materials handling and scheduling is the third area which falls under "Production". With the advent of computer aided systems, successful creative strategies have, for example, included just-in-time inventory control systems (JIT) and materials requirement planning (MRP). JIT and MRP are used to bring raw materials in only when needed, not too soon and not too late. These processes were designed to reduce the cost of carrying inventory. In addition, companies are now using "quality circles", allowing employees to input their ideas on how best to have materials flow through the plant. With the development of e-business techniques, creative ideas are being considered all the time.

Quality Control and Control

Quality control and control is the final option within the Production area of the strategic palette. There are several types of quality control approaches. A few examples are: statistical quality control, where only a small percentage of the finished goods is checked; automated quality control, where the production machines themselves have built-in sensory devices which constantly check output; and, of course, the old-fashioned method still in use in some factories, where each product is individually checked. These approaches measure the quality of our outputs; usable vs. rejects. People would be amazed to learn of the number of rejects that occur and are accepted by management. There is a multibillion dollar industry within the steel industry that thrives by buying and selling reduced priced mill rejects. Also, factory seconds and outlet stores are in this category.

It is not hard to imagine the devastating effects that occur when manufacturing companies produce unacceptable products. Not only do they lose their customers because the products are unreliable, but the cost of the products that are produced with some quality goes out of sight. When it takes two attempts to make one product, costs escalate because labor doubles, material costs almost double and overhead costs increase drastically. The better quality control you have and the better strategically placed you are, the greater the likelihood that you will be a successful company.

It is not only important to control quality, but the entire organization and all of its processes. All members of the organization have to be in the right place at the right time, with the right training and tools for the organization to be effective. There are hundreds of creative, successful techniques that are currently being used in this area. Ever hear of TQM (Total Quality Management) and CQI (Continuous Quality Improvement)? If you are to be a successful competitor you must consider these areas of the strategic palette very carefully and creatively.

Research and Development (R & D)

1) PRODUCT > Lead/Follow

2) PROCESS > Lead/Follow

Research and Development, another area on the strategic palette, is also very important to gain a successful competitive advantage, especially in today's advanced technological society. There are two basic strategic categories here: Product Development and Process Development. Each can take a leader or follower position.

Product or Process

Researching the product is one option for you. You could focus your research on the product area in marketing to make it better, bigger, faster, quicker, or smoother. However, there are some products that cannot be changed, especially industrial products, which often have to be made to detailed specifications. For example, in the oil industry, there are products that are used to pump oil out of the ground called sucker rods. These rods must meet certain specifications set by the American Petroleum Institute. Although rods could be different, they would not be of much value if they failed to meet API standards. A successful R&D approach then might be to focus on process innovation instead of product innovation. I once was part of a company that, through research, developed a way to modify a machine used in another industry for the production of sucker rods. Prior to our company's machine modification, rods were made on machines called turret lathes. It took several minutes to make a rod on this type of machine. Our company took a machine for screw manufacturing and modified it to make sucker rods. As a result, we could produce a rod in several seconds, not minutes. Before we could barely get into production, a big company bought us out so they could have the technology. Within a year we turned a $300,000 investment into $3,000,000. Researching the process and finding a way to produce more efficiently often leads to success.

Lead or Follow

For each product or process approach, another aspect to consider is to lead or follow. You could be the one to invent the new product or process, or you could be the one to look at the new product or process and improve it. There are strategic advantages to both leading and following. Generally, it is advantageous to be the product or process innovator because you are the first in the marketplace. Being first obviously puts you in the lead and it is difficult to displace the leader from the marketplace since it requires a large amount of resources.

In their book *Marketing Warfare*, Reiss and Trout compare military strategy to business strategy. The lead or follow analogy goes as follows. In wartime, it is very difficult to win using a straight frontal attack on an entrenched enemy. The reason this is true is because the defenders are positioned and waiting for the enemy. They know where all the obstacles are, have their communications network in place, and so they wait. When the enemy does attack, who do you think has the advantage?

It takes a lot to overcome forces that have held and secured the ground for some time. The conventional wisdom is that attackers using a frontal assault need at least three times the resources as the defenders. The same is true in the business world. If you are entrenched as the market leader, other businesses need significantly more resources to get ahead of you. Therefore, the leader in the marketplace has the advantage.

However, there are also some disadvantages to being the leader. The leader goes through all the rough terrain first and makes the costly mistakes. Those who follow can observe and learn and not make the same mistakes. Also, there is always the chance that the innovative product or process will lead to a costly failure.

Just as there are pros and cons in taking the leader approach, there are lots of pros and cons in taking the follower position. The main disadvantage, as illustrated, is that you forfeit a strong position by not assuming the leader strategy. The main advantage is the diminished risk you take by being a follower. In many instances, it is acceptable to be the follower as long as you have a large resource advantage over any potential leaders. In addition, there are effective strategies that can be used against a leader. Using the military analogy, if your army could not overcome an entrenched enemy you still have several options that would facilitate your victory. For example, you could flank the enemy (meaning coming in from the side), an approach used by the Japanese when they took on the American automotive industry. Instead of entering the market with a full line of vehicles, they elected to make fuel efficient, smaller, less expensive automobiles; a market of little interest to American producers. The Japanese subsequently captured the fuel efficient, more reliable compact car market, obtaining a beachhead in the U.S. auto marketplace. Gradually, their cars became less efficient and a little more costly. Now they are sitting right in the middle of the marketplace holding a major share.

On your palette under Research and Development there are many strategies in product and process innovation for both leading and following. Again, you must be creative. Reiss and Trout were quite creative with their warfare analogy. You can be too.

Management Information Systems (MIS)

1) HARDWARE & SOFTWARE
2) INFORMATION DISTRIBUTION

Management Information Systems (MIS) is the fourth area on the "competitive" side of your palette. It is not an area often thought of for achieving a competitive advantage, but now as the new paradigm shift of e-business takes hold, it is becoming more and more important. The two areas under MIS are hardware and software and information distribution.

Hardware and Software

There are two basic tools for management information systems; hardware and software. Hardware is the equipment you operate with, and software is the programming that allows you to process information. The right combination of hardware and software, appropriate to your line of business, and used in a unique creative manner, can facilitate your position as a successful competitor.

Much can be written about the new hardware that drives today's management information system. First there were large mainframes, then came the minicomputers, and now we are in an area of server networks and work stations. As the software gets more complex, appropriate hardware must be installed in order to maximize the software's potential.

In today's high-tech environment software "systems" are changing on an almost daily basis. Successful companies are constantly updating their software in a way that facilitates the integrative team approach now being used in successful companies. The big buzz today is "e-business", where companies are focused on inter and intranet development. Companies are moving to obtain a competitive edge by developing a close interconnected relationship between their suppliers and customers, utilizing e-business web technology.

Information Distribution

Effective distribution of the information gathered can be extremely important to your company. Making sure the right people have the right information at the right time is a way to be more competitive. A well known travel agency is an example of a company that exhibits effective information distribution.

This once small travel agency, formed in 1945, has grown into one of the largest travel agencies in the British market. At the end of 1990, this travel agency upgraded its computerized management information system as a basis for a comprehensive automated information delivery system that permits the detailed analysis and planning of travel needs. This system does not just print out the travel information, it graphically shows it. The travel agency was introduced to the Cognos PC-based package PowerPlay. It turned out to be exactly the type of system to match the needs of its travel division. All of its offices have a sophisticated point-of-sale system linked to the computer reservations systems for air travel, hotels, and car rental. These systems also print tickets, brochures, invoices, and itineraries. The travel agency gets 97% of that information electronically at the point of sale and transmits it after validation for storage on a computer that holds the client database. Before this little company became involved in this new system, it was data rich but information poor. A lot of decisions were made based on estimations and experience. The travel agency and its customers can now have access to high quality management information at the click of a mouse. They provide high quality management information on paper and also help customers to analyze trends to manage their travel allowance more efficiently because it is colorful, easy to understand and fast. They are able to demonstrate all the travel options to prospective customers on laptop computers, which have given them the competitive advantage in winning and retaining business. Now, they also supply the PowerPlay package to larger organizations that are interested. By doing this, they can send their corporate clients monthly reports on diskette for analysis by the client's own travel manager. They are developing a system to deliver this internationally. This will enable the transfer of statistics to a customer directly or to the branch for the customer to collect.

Another company that uses information effectively is The Limited. The Limited is a leader in women's clothing; it has the ability to know what is going on in all the stores at all times. For instance, a product that is located in the bottom left hand corner window in five stores is moving well, but it is slow in the other stores where it is located in the back. Using this information, the other stores could move that product to a similar location. Also, they are able to track a particular product moving on the East Coast but not on the West Coast. They then can bring the product where it is selling the best. They are moving inventory around both internally and externally.

This is primarily the reason for the success of The Limited; they are creatively controlling their inventory through management information systems.

There are now countless stories about companies initiating new e-business technologies. It has become obvious that unless you can "paint" well in these areas, you may not only lose your competitive advantage, but you may or will lose your company as well.

As computer technology continues to change, more and more companies will be striving for a competitive advantage in this area. If you are to be successful, you must consider this part of your strategic palette.

Human Resource Management (HRM)

1) STAFFING
2) MOTIVATION AND LEADERSHIP

With the advent of downsizing and with an increased understanding of employee bottom line impact, Human Resource Management (HRM) is receiving more attention as a strategic tool. It focuses on the people in the organization, looking at issues related to staffing, leadership, and motivation.

Staffing

Staffing includes the use of methods that allow companies to recruit and select the best person for the job. This issue is even more complex today because of affirmative action.

HRM also involves developing and maintaining those who are hired. Well trained employees who can handle multiple jobs and understand the latest technology can provide you with that competitive edge.

Labor relations, unions and all other job related issues are part of Human Resource Management falling under the "Staffing" area. If you know how to incorporate the union as a strategic partner instead of considering it as a necessary evil, you could be successful where others are not.

Motivation and Leadership

If you are to be competitive, it is necessary to successfully motivate and lead employees. There are many techniques available that help managers become more affective leaders and even more techniques available that assist in developing a motivated work force. Some of these techniques include addressing employees' basic needs, bonuses, pay raises, and participation in decision-making. One approach that receives lot of attention is team development where employees are offered an opportunity to voice their opinions and input their ideas. The following are some real world examples of creative motivation and leadership.

Wal-Mart is a human resource management success story. Their story is based on the relationship Wal-Mart's managers have with employees in the stores and in the distribution centers. The manner in which managers deal with their employees is often reflected in the employee's treatment of the customer. Treating the customers right brings them back, and a strong loyal customer base can be the foundation of a successful business.

It could be argued that the smartest motivational strategic move Wal-Mart ever made was to give its employees more equitable treatment in the company. Starting a profit-sharing plan for all the employees was the first big step. Every employee that has worked for the company at least one year and works at least one thousand hours a year becomes eligible for the plan. A formula based on profit growth is used to contribute a percentage of every eligible employee's wages to his or her plan. They can take this percentage of wages when they leave the company, in cash or Wal-Mart stock.

Financial partnership programs were also started at Wal-Mart. One program, an employee stock-purchase plan, allows employees to buy stock through payroll deductions at a discount off market value. These and other motivational techniques work. Wal-Mart realized that fair and equitable treatment of employees and its motivation techniques in action promote team player attitudes. Their success under Human resource management is apparent as exhibited by their continued expansion.

Human resource success stories are not new. One of the major factors in the success of Ben & Jerry's occurred ten years ago, when they were an up-and-coming company. Their story was illustrated in the January 1992 issue of *Personnel Journal*. It was about Ben & Jerry's "small company with a big heart". Ben & Jerry's created a socially responsible company. A company not only socially responsible to society, but to its workforce as well. It has developed human resource management programs that improve the quality of life for employees. Some of these programs include opinion surveys, tuition reimbursement, flexible spending accounts, evaluate-your-boss polls, paid health club fees, maternity, paternity and adoption leave with partial pay, and child care centers. Free cholesterol and blood pressure testing and body and foot massages are available through a wellness plan.

Ben & Jerry's is concerned with internally and externally giving back to the community. The company is always trying to come up with new benefits and programs to include everyone. For example, employees' unmarried domestic partners are covered under its health care plan. A short-term disability program was also created. This program allows for employees to receive 100% of their salary for six weeks and 60% for six months until long-term disability coverage begins. The company also reimburses employees' adoption costs and caps them at the cost of a normal hospital delivery. Ben & Jerry's challenges itself, its employees, and its vendors to give something back to the community. It also reflects a commitment to minority and female representation. As a result, Ben & Jerry's people have a more favorable view of their jobs, supervision, and their company than do employees from American companies in general.

The importance of good human resource management cannot be overstated. Don't forget this part of your palette when "painting" your successful company.

Finance

(1) CASH FLOW
(2) CASH HANDLING

This area of the strategic palette differs from the "financial strategy" area on the side of the palette where "allocation strategies" are located. Finance involves two options that can help you to be more competitive. These options have been labeled cash flow and cash handling.

Cash Flow

It is important to handle your cash well if you are to succeed in business. The survivability of your company when it is new or in tough times can often depend upon your ability in this area. One example of a successful cash flow strategy is illustrated by a company that requires its customers to pay cash on delivery (COD) and at the same time gets its suppliers to grant them 90 days to pay. What this amounts to is an interest free loan. A loan that is available even when one is not available from the bank. Often these "interest free" loans come at a time when the company is in deep trouble and needs it the most. Creative successful planners frequently take advantage of cash flow strategies.

Cash Handling

Cash handling is what you actually do with the cash on hand. It is the ability to move cash around the organization. This is becoming more important as we deal in the international arena, where the use of multiple currencies has become part of everyday operations. An example of an international cash handling strategy that has gone wrong would be if you were to buy some equipment from Germany for $1,000,000 US dollars, and sell it to someone in the United States for $1,500,000 US dollars. Your profit should be $500,000. You agree to pay for the equipment when it is ready in six months, however, you agree to pay in German currency. In six months when the equipment is ready, you bring your $1,000,000 US dollars to a German bank to exchange it for German currency. However, you discover that the exchange rate has changed and you can now only get half as much German currency as you could six months ago. You now need $2,000,000 US dollars to buy the equipment. As a result, the $500,000 profit turns into a $500,000 loss. A creative planner would have developed a strategy such as currency hedging, to reduce this kind of risk.

There are many other areas where cash handling can become a factor. Another example would be neglecting to deposit cash into interest bearing accounts. Successful companies are careful with cash.

Johnson & Johnson is an example of a successful company using effective cash handling. Johnson & Johnson Co. needed better control of its cash. It had to take three steps to make effective use of their corporate cash: reduce bank credit risk, improve the flow of cash through the corporation, and establish an international coordination center to streamline the flow of funds throughout their operations worldwide. Its managers began focusing on bank credit risks ten years ago. After considerable research, a system was developed to monitor exposure and a policy to reduce or eliminate unnecessary risk was established. It analyzed its exposure by bank and by dollar amount. The exposure was divided into four categories, cash management exposure, overt investment in a bank, transaction exposure, and contractual exposure. Then, it had to learn where the exposure was. Rating agencies helped to give them a broad perspective. Johnson and Johnson also established an internal credit watch report that is updated weekly. Statistical analysis from the rating agencies on client banks is used every six months. After its exposure was examined, a policy was established. Daily cash management is the first category in the policy. The objective of the other three categories is to have zero losses from any transaction, which is critical in determining how conservative or aggressive they are going to be.

Also, the Cash Management Improvement Program (CMIP) was created to supplement Johnson & Johnson's credit quality policy. It is a two-year program that was created to improve cash flow, eliminate unnecessary balances and costs, and reduce bank credit exposure as a side effect. Johnson & Johnson had five lead banks with standard collection and disbursement services. Since the subsidiaries controlled much of the process, they had no way of knowing how much money was coming or going. Johnson & Johnson is a decentralized organization, but it had to centralize its treasury function as much as possible. Today, the CMIP focuses on two types of flow, the actual flow of the money and the flow of information that enables them to manage the money. The company eliminated local payroll accounts and as many local depositories as possible, which resulted in one lead bank that provides concentration, funds transfer, and disbursement services. The most time consuming part of the process was replacing the local payroll accounts with direct deposit or controlled disbursement checking accounts. The effect of the Cash Management Improvement Program was to reduce the number of banks and balances. Bank cost management has become more effective because of the low balances. Low balances mean that companies pay fees and control their expenditures more carefully. Johnson & Johnson also reduced its bank exposure, increasing their efficiency and communication.

The third and final step of Johnson and Johnson's plan was to achieve tax-efficient intercompany lending and cash-efficient worldwide netting. To do this, Johnson & Johnson had to establish a Belgian Coordination Center (BCC). BCC loans money to other Johnson & Johnson subsidiaries throughout the world. Basically, the Center makes one transaction for each currency on a specified date each month. BCC also eliminates third-party borrowing and dividends being subject to a withholding tax. BCC is able to recycle cash.

Each portion of the three-part program had contributed to greater efficiency. Tracking bank performance helped reduce bank credit risk. The two-year Cash Management Improvement Program helped improve the flow of cash throughout the corporation. Finally, the Belgian Coordination Center served to streamline the international flow of funds. The success of managing cash at Johnson & Johnson depends on this integrated effort. Obviously, Johnson and Johnson was able to creatively use this part of the strategic palette.

Organizational Design

(1) STRUCTURE
(2) COMMUNICATION

All of the previous competitive options are circumscribed by Organizational Design. Organizational Design is the design of the entire organization to facilitate the action within these units. It consists of two parts: Structure and Communication.

Structure

The structure of a company is the way it is set up. It can be defined as the framework that supports the organization's processes. One area of structure is hierarchical structure. It shows the vertical chain of command and the horizontal span of control. There are basically four types of hierarchical structures. They include simple, functional, divisional, and matrix. These will be discussed in more detail in Chapter 3: Environmental Scanning.

But, there is much more to structure than hierarchical reporting and control. Structure includes such things as how the organization is physically laid out. It includes both physical relationships and interrelationships. You can see that if your company is to be successful, you must find the best structure, perhaps one that has not typically been used in your industry before.

Communication

Communication within the structure is the network that links all of the functional areas together. Communication is very important in an organization, as it is becoming more necessary for companies to work together as a team. Without communication, there is confusion and misunderstanding. It truly improves efficiency. There are hundreds of communication strategies. Paint one of your own.

Summary

In order to determine how to be successful in today's highly competitive business environment you are going to have to "paint", to be creative and unique and discover better ways to assure the long-term viability of your company. If you want to be a prosperous successful painter then the first thing you have to do is lay out your palette in an effective and efficient manner.

An effective and efficient strategic palette layout starts with two basic areas. The first area is resource allocation strategies and the second is competitive strategies. Allocation strategies include the use of financial models, portfolio models, and combinations of both. Financial models help to optimally allocate resources using financial data to compare each product, product line, or business unit individually. However, the problem with financial models is that they do not consider the interrelationships between products, product lines, or business units. Portfolio models do consider these relationships. They utilize some measure of the industry outlook and some measure of your competitive capabilities within that industry. They consider synergy, which is two or more units working together producing a sum greater than their individual parts.

The competitive side of your palette is laid out by dividing it into common sense based areas that were described by their function within the organization. These areas include: marketing, production, research and development, human resource management, management information systems, finance, and organization design. Using marketing, you can become successful by making aspects of the product, price, promotion and distribution better or unique.

Production, another area on the "competitive" side of the strategic palette, includes facilities and location, processes and capacity, materials handling and scheduling, and quality control and control. Next is research and development, showing how an organization can be more competitive by changing the product or process and by leading or following using hardware and software and information distribution. Ben and Jerry's and Wal-Mart are examples of how you can be more competitive through human resource management, since these companies have become well known for their HRM expertise. Staffing and motivation and leadership are the two options under HRM. Another area where a company can become more competitive and increase its probability of winning is finance. Johnson and Johnson illustrated how it gets a handle on their cash flows and cash handling, making the company more profitable. The last area on the strategic palette is organizational design, which encompasses all of the functional areas above. Organizational design covers structure and communication.

Your palette has been laid out in front of you. It contains the source for *every* possible strategic option you can have to be more competitive and successful. Everything you can think of can be extracted somewhere from this palette. Exploring your organization allows you to think about possibilities and how to incorporate the tools given to you. Now, it is time to paint. But where do you start? You will learn where and how next.

Chapter 2

Getting Started: The Strategic Planning Process

Now that your palette is in front of you and ready to go, to be a successful painter you must have a technique or process which allows you to use the paints on your palette in a creative manner. This technique should allow you to "paint" in a manner that enables you to truly express your unique creative talent. For example, the painter's technique usually starts with laying in the background and when appropriate, locating and placing the horizon. After that, the main elements of the picture are put into place. Although not impossible, it would be very difficult and probably lead to a poor painting if he or she would proceed in a different manner. This does not mean that a great painting is not possible with a different approach, but the probability for success is significantly diminished without good technique. The same is true when developing creative successful business strategies.

In business, like painting, the successful manager or entrepreneur is trying to create a unique and successful product. Therefore, successful business strategies require a technique which allows the manager or entrepreneur to use the strategic pallet in a creative productive manner. In business, this technique is referred to as the strategic planning process. As in painting, this process is no guarantee of success, but it will increase the probability of developing unique and successful strategic and problem solutions for your business; ones that convey your individuality and ingenuity.

Although there are several different types of strategic planning processes, we are going to use a generic or a compiled version of these processes. One that will enable us to express our individual creativity in an effective and efficient manner. One that will ensure the highest probability of success.

However, before this planning system is introduced, it is important that you have a clear understanding of what the strategic planning process can and can not do for you and your organization. Since the ultimate objective of "painting" is to create a successful organization with longevity, a good strategic planning process should successfully enable you to:

1. Change the direction of the company (when necessary) by reviewing and auditing present activities. This will allow you to make proper adjustments and modifications in light of changing environment and company aims.

2. Accelerate growth and improve profitability.

3. Weed out poor performers among divisions; concentrate on strategies that can lead to success.

4. Raise strategic issues for top management consideration including long-term and short-range operating plans (i.e. reference for budgets).

5. Develop better information through continuous effective training with which managers can make better decisions.

6. Develop better coordination of activities by gaining more effective control of operations.

7. Develop a sense of security among managers and company employees by providing understanding and awareness in reference to the changing environment and the company's ability to adapt to it. This can only be achieved by effective communications between organizational units and personnel throughout the company.

8. Pick up the pace of a "tired" company; guide divisions and research personnel in developing new products and allocate assets to areas of best potential.

9. Develop a Mission Statement, which will serve as a road map showing the company's direction and strategy in getting there. Set challenging, yet realistic and attainable objectives.

A good planning process can help you accomplish more than one of these tasks. For example, a large diversified firm may find that the need to coordinate plans among divisions is particularly urgent. These items are not mutually exclusive, some are subsets of others and many are closely interrelated.

The Strategic Planning Process

All planning processes or systems, regardless of whether or not they are artistic, technical, business or personal have the same general layout. First, they must define the problem. Then they must set some specific goals, gather pertinent information, develop a plan to achieve their goals, consider implementation, monitor the system chosen, and finally, analyze feedback data to make any corrections and adjustments. The planning system we are going to use is no different as it contains the following elements:

1. MISSION STATEMENT
2. GOALS & OBJECTIVES
3. ENVIRONMENTAL SCANNING
4. STRATEGY FORMULATION
5. IMPLEMENTATION
6. MONITORING & CONTROLLING
7. FEEDBACK
   (See Figure. 2.1)

The creative artist uses the same process in the following manner. First he or she sets the painting's parameters. This is often done by locating the painting's horizon. If the horizon is located near the bottom of the picture, then the artist will probably require lots of blues and whites. The painter does not have to concern him/herself with lots of green and brown. On the other hand, if the horizon is located near the top, the artist needs to focus on just the opposite. In business, defining the parameters is requires a "mission statement". More will be said on mission statements later in this chapter.

Once the parameters of the picture are developed, the artist must then decide what he/she is trying to accomplish. In other words, what feeling, emotion, or impression are they trying to communicate to the viewer. These are their goals. Businesses must also set goals. More will also be said about this at the end of this chapter.

The Strategic Planning Process

Figure 2.1

Next, the artist needs to understand what they are capable of and what is out there that can help them accomplish their goals. They may elect for example, to review what other artists have done and explore the availability of different types of brushes and paints. In business planning, this is called "environmental scanning". Chapter 3 will address this task.

Once this is done, the next step is to develop a specific plan for achieving the stated goals. For example, if the goal of the artist is to illustrate the sadness within a particular person, the artist may chose to paint his/her picture using dark running colors. The business equivalent to this is the phase of the strategic planning process called "strategy formulation", which is discussed in Chapters 4, 5, and 6.

But before you can start to paint, you must have a plan to map out what to do when. This is the "implementation" element of the strategic planning process and is presented in Chapter 7.

I'm sure you have all seen artists standing back to look at their work. It is obvious that they are appraising the progress of their work and seeing if it is turning out the way they expected. They, just like the successful planners, are "monitoring and controlling" their progress. If they discover a mistake, they make the corrections through "feedback". We will look closer at this in Chapter 8.

If the process is basically the same for all artists, as well as all strategic planners, what are the sources of differences that set apart successful paintings and winning strategies? If each painter and planner uses the same proper palette layout and the effective and efficient incorporation of a good process, then the answer is the individual's creativity.

Crown Cork and Seal Company presents a classic case that illustrates the value of creativity coupled with an effective strategic planning process. Some time ago, when J. F. Connely became president, the company was on the verge of bankruptcy, with only a small part of its product line (bottle caps and related closures) earning a modest profit. The outlook for its major business, tin cans, was dismal. Product demand was not increasing at a significant level because glass, paper, and plastics were making inroads into the market. Competitors had excess capacity, and price competition was severe. But there were a few bright spots in the total picture, and Connely decided to concentrate on one of these. After careful environmental scanning, Connely discovered that cans that could hold contents under pressure were more difficult to make and consequently were not subject to cutthroat competition. Moreover, the growth prospects for these were better than average, with aerosols and beer being the major users. As for beer containers, Connely predicted that metal cans would take market share from glass bottles. Thus, after reviewing the company's mission statement, he set serving this special niche as Crown Cork's goal.

After continuing his external analysis and conducting an internal analysis of the company, several major strategies were formulated for the purpose of obtaining a competitive advantage in this niche. On the allocation side of his "palette" all thought of a full line was abandoned and the regular can business was liquidated. This provided some capital to pacify the bankers. On the competitive side of his "palette", Connely wanted to give excellent service to his selected customers. This involved locating plants close to customers, installing some new equipment, and organizing a communication and distribution process which allowed for customer needs to be meet effectively and efficiently. In addition, overhead was trimmed far below the industry average.

The results at Crown Cork were dramatic. As predicted, volume grew much faster in this segment than in the total can industry, not only in beer but later in soft drinks as well. Crown Cork's focus on service enabled it to obtain an increasing share of this volume. Meanwhile, the low overhead gave the company the best profit margin in the industry. It can be argued that it would have been almost impossible to carry out this complex maneuver with out some sort of plan. Today, successful companies are doing the same thing.

As a consultant, I have often been told that planning is not necessary. I have heard managers say, "we just don't have the time to develop a plan," or "things are changing too fast for us to plan." What these people do not know is that the chance for success in today's competitive environment is almost non-existent without a good strategic plan. The winning coach of the Super Bowl did not say that he did not have time to develop a plan. He did not say that there was no sense in planning, since things would change as soon as the game went on. What do you think the probability of success would be if they entered the stadium without a plan? So, like the successful coach or painter, successful outcomes are highly correlated to good planning, and good planning incorporates a good, common sense planning process.

Mission Statements

The mission statement has been given many different labels. It has been referred to as a creed statement, statement of purpose, statement of philosophies, statement of beliefs, statement of business principles, or vision statement. Sometimes it is just thought of as a statement that defines the business. A mission statement reveals the long-term (long-term being 2 to 5 years) vision of an organization. It can often be found in the front or back cover of annual reports, displayed throughout a firm's premises, and distributed with company information that is sent to constituencies. The mission statement is a part of numerous internal reports, such as loan requests, supplier agreements, labor relation contracts, business plans and customer service agreements. However, none of the above really addresses the issue of what a mission statement is and how it should be used.

Many organizations spend large sums of money and time to establish objectives and implement strategies, but they often overlook developing a purposeful mission statement. It has been estimated that approximately 40% of large corporations in America have not yet developed a formal mission statement. However, many companies have started to realize their value, and the number of companies with formal mission statements is rapidly increasing.

The current thought on mission statements is based largely on guidelines set forth in the mid 1970's by Peter Drucker, who is often called the "father of modern management". Drucker believes that asking the question, "what is our business?" is synonymous with asking the question, "what is our mission?". He claims that it is an enduring statement of purpose that distinguishes one organization from similar enterprises. In simpler terms, the mission statement is a declaration of an organization's reason for being.

Nevertheless, there still seems to be a lot of confusion as to what a mission statement is. Most mission statements wind up being either propaganda speeches put out by senior management to convince the shareholders how wonderful things are, or they are nothing more than a series of professed goals. However, it is important to remember that the mission statement is the first step in the strategic planning process. Its purpose therefore, is to set the parameters of a creative winning strategy. It should help us paint the picture by, for example, locating the horizon. Obviously, it would be difficult to develop a successful painting without first laying out the canvas. It should be just as obvious that organizations must first determine who they are before a successful strategy can be developed. To this end, a purposeful mission statement should respond to the following four questions:

1. What is our business or who are we?
2. Who are our customers or whom do we serve?
3. What are the needs of those we serve?
4. How do we fulfill these needs?

Importance of Mission Statements

A good example of the importance of mission statements is illustrated by looking at the results of a study comparing mission statements of the Fortune 500 firms. The study concluded that high performers had more comprehensive mission statements than low performers.

The importance of a mission statement can be further stressed by the example of the W.T. Grant retail chain. In 1975, W.T. Grant went bankrupt. Prior to that it had almost 2 billion dollars in sales and 1,000 stores. But, they did not know what business they were in. The executives could not make up their minds if the stores should be full service stores like J.C. Penney and Sears or a discounter such as Kmart. They settled on falling somewhere between the two and ended up standing for nothing. This is one of the reasons they consequently went bankrupt. Although, this failure occurred over 25 years ago, companies have still not learned of the importance of a good mission statement.

Developing a Mission Statement

A clear mission statement is needed before alternative strategies can be formulated and implemented. It is important to involve as many managers as possible in the process because, through involvement, people seem to become more committed to the organization, develop a better understanding regarding what the organization is all about, and generally add insight to the discussion.

A widely used approach to developing a mission statement is to first ask all managers to read as background information selected articles about mission statements. Then managers are asked to personally prepare a mission statement for the organization. A facilitator, a committee of the managers or, in the case of a small business, the owner of the company, then merges these statements into a single document and distributes this draft mission statement to all managers, requesting modifications and additions. A meeting is then called to revise the document.

During the process of developing a mission statement, some organizations use discussion groups made up of managers to make developments and modifications. Some organizations hire an outside consultant or facilitator to manage the process and help draft the language. Decisions on how best to communicate the mission statement to all managers, employees, and external constituencies are needed when the document is in final form. Some organizations even develop a videotape to explain the mission statement and how it was developed. It is thought that an emotional bond develops when an individual personally identifies with the underlying values and behavior of a firm, thus turning intellectual agreement and commitment into a sense of mission. With these concepts in mind, let us now discuss the four basic questions that must be answered in the mission statement.

What is Our Business, or Who Are We?

This seems like a straightforward and simple question, but it may well be the deciding factor of the future stability of the organization. Yet, you would be amazed at how many companies could not answer that question. Who are we, what is our business, and what business are we in are not questions to be addressed only at the initial stages of the company. On the contrary, it is just as important to address these questions when the company is successful, for often companies lose their way after the first taste of success.

Defining the business or organization is a complex task. It cannot be overly restrictive since that would run the risk of inducing shortsightedness. On the other hand, it cannot be too general because without some degree of focus, the organization may not be affective. Such organizations may wander from one opportunity to another causing their managers to spend inordinate amounts of time analyzing what could be done, without actually doing much of anything. In order to answer the question "who are we?," managers must reach a difficult balance between being too restrictive and providing guidelines that are too general and, therefore, unclear.

Managers who carefully consider what business they are in often reach new insights about their organization. Insights that can change the strategic management of the firm. For example, let us look at United Airlines. What is their business? If the response is transporting people, then the definition is too narrow since that would eliminate them from exploring such business opportunities as over-night mail, packages and other types of freight. On the other hand, if the response is the transportation business, then the parameters are too broad and they would have a difficult time trying to focus on what they do best. Under this definition, they could be looking into owning truck lines or railroads. Perhaps a better definition would be that they are in the air transportation business.

A consultant who was called into a company to help develop a strategic plan told me a good mission statement story. Of course, the first step was to develop a mission statement and the first step in this process, as we have discussed, is determining what business the company is in. When the consultant asked this question of management their response was that they were in the micro-encapsulation business. Not knowing exactly what this was, the consultant asked for a further explanation. What the company did, said one manager, was to encapsulate molecules. For example, they encapsulated a molecule of eye makeup so that when it was rubbed onto the skin, it would penetrate the persons cells and thereby remove wrinkles. So, says the consultant, you are in the cosmetic industry. The manager agreed, but continued by saying that they also used the same process to encapsulate molecules of fragrance to be used in printing for "scratch me" ads, where you rub the page and the fragrance is released. The consultant then responded by saying, "Okay, in addition to the cosmetic business, you are also in the special print business, right?" Once again, the manager agreed, but continued by saying that they also encapsulated pharmaceuticals so they could be "timed released." The consultant was still not phased. He responded by saying that there was no problem with being in several different businesses, as long as each was defined. He asked if there were any other businesses that they were in. The answer was, "No that's it."

As the consultant was returning to the conference room after lunch, he noticed that, although there seemed to be a lot of rooms and a lot of people walking around, no production facilities were in sight. When the meeting was called to order he asked where production took place. One manager replied, saying that they did not have any production capabilities. "What do you mean?," asked the consultant. The manager said, "We don't produce anything, all we do is advise our customers on how to do the micro-encapsulation." Well then, said the consultant, you are not in the cosmetic business, the special printing business, or the pharmaceutical business. What you are in is the research and development business. "Yes, yes, that's it", replied all the managers. So it took a consultant and all the company's managers half a day to discover the answer to that seemingly simple question, "what is our business?"

You can imagine the consequences of developing a strategic plan without knowing what business you're in. In the consultant's case, a competitive strategic plan could have been developed for the cosmetic industry, the special printing industry, the pharmaceutical industry, or all three. It would, at best, done nothing for the company and. at worst, led to their downfall. There is a big difference between winning strategies for R & D firms and those in cosmetics, printing, or pharmaceutical.

So, don't take the task of defining what business you're in too lightly. It is very important, can be quite revealing, and can be very difficult to do.

Who Are Our Customers Or Who Do We Serve?

Answering this question correctly can save a company loads of money and other resources and it will further define the company's parameters. It can be very costly if you do not know if your customers are men or women, local or foreign, consumers or governments. For example, when it comes to advertising, the company will face a lot of difficulties, resulting in a waste of financial resources.

How can you determine who are your customers? First, it depends on to whom you are marketing your products. For instance, Johnson and Johnson states in their mission statement, "We believe our first responsibility is to Doctors, Nurses, Patients, to Mothers, and all others who use our products and services." Therefore, the focus of their strategy must be directed at doctors, nurses, patients and mothers. However, you could ask why should they consider mothers when their products are baby care goods? Aren't their customers babies? But after a little consideration, it is easy to see that it isn't the baby who buys their products, but the person who looks after the baby. In other words, in most cases, it is the baby's mother. So, it is to her that they market their products. That is why mothers are specified in their mission statement.

What Are the Needs of Those We Serve?

A good mission statement reflects the needs of its customers. Rather than developing a product and then trying to find a market, the operating philosophies of organizations should be to identify customer needs and then provide a product or service to fulfill those needs. An organization should identify the utility of that product to its customers. That is why AT&T has a mission statement that focuses on communication rather than telephones. Exxon's mission statement focuses on energy rather than oil or gas. Union Pacific's mission statement focuses on transportation rather than railroads, and Universal Studio's focus is on entertainment rather than movies.

It very important to remember however, that products are not needs. If you say that your customer's need is Coca-cola, you could eliminate any other kind of beverage as a product. On the other hand, if you say that your customer's need is a refreshing drink, then you can meet their need with Coke, other flavored soft drinks, juices, etc. That might save you a lot of trouble and market share when other companies try to pre-empt your market position by trying to sell their non-carbonated drinks in your market place.

Be smart, be creative. If you consider needs to be products, then you constrain creativity. Products are there to meet needs. Another example would be the automobile industry. You probably should state that you are in the transportation business rather than the business of making cars. Making cars is too restrictive, especially if you make Ferraris. Although a Ferrari provides transportation, the question is whether the Ferrari customer buys a Ferrari simply for transportation, or for the image and an ego boost.

The following are some guidelines that you might want to consider when trying to determine what the needs are of those you serve. If you are in the garment business, your customers' needs aren't necessarily clothing, but attractive looks. If you produce shoes, you are perhaps selling comfort to the feet, attractive looks or simply walking pleasure, rather than just shoes. We can offer security, comfort and a place that is clean and happy rather than just a house. You are selling knowledge and hours of entertainment when you sell a book. You sell leisure and the sound of music when you sell a CD. The efficient use of the buyers' skills is realized when you sell a simple tool.

As Peter Drucker would say, "It is the customer who determines what a business is. It is the customer alone whose willingness to pay for a good or service converts economic resources into wealth and things into goods. What we think we produce is of no importance, especially to the future of the business and its success. So what the customer buys and considers a value is never a product, it is always a utility, meaning what that product or service does for him. The customer is the foundation of the business and keeps it in existence".

There is a distinct difference between what people want and what people actually need. Firms should try to understand this and focus on this because fulfilling a need of a consumer is as close to a guaranteed successful business as you can get.

How Do We Meet These Needs?

Many companies overlook this aspect of the mission statement because it is more like stating the company's goals and objectives. But it is vital that we include this in the mission statement, as it forms an important part of the company's strategies. Do you manufacture or distribute? What exactly does your organization do to meet the needs of its customers? For instance, Stop and Shop meets the needs of its patrons by being right in the neighborhood so that groceries and other items needed on a day to day basis are easily accessible. They understand the need of their customers who have sudden urges to buy certain items, and those consumers who are unable to shop during daylight. Therefore, by keeping their outlets open 24 hours a day, they reach a segment of customers that they could not have reached before.

When looking at how you meet your customers' needs, look at what you are doing now, not what you will be doing in the future. This will serve as a starting point when you are developing your strategies.

Evaluating Mission Statements

Let us now take a look at the mission statements used at one time or another by some companies and evaluate them according to our requirements.

Ford Motor Company

"Ford Motor Company is a worldwide leader in automotive and automotive-related products and services as well as in newer industries, such as aerospace, communications, and financial services. Our mission is to improve continually our products and services to meet our customers' needs, allowing us to prosper as a business and to provide a reasonable return to our stockholders, the owners of our business."

This statement gives us an understanding of what business they are in. But, they haven't specified who their customers are, which could be because they manufacture cars for all those who have the capacity to drive. However, since they have gone into newer industries such as aerospace, communications, and financial services, it is vital that they define their customers. If they do not do this, they will loose focus and miss out on a market segment in which they could have been successful, and they could end up wasting significant resources.

Although they have taken into consideration the customers needs and they hope to improve their products and services to meet those needs, there is no mention of how they hope to achieve this. Instead, they have taken into consideration their stockholders. It is not necessary to mention providing reasonable return for stockholders because this is an unsaid responsibility of all public companies. This concern is unimportant to the customers. Account statements will be more than adequate to satisfy the stockholders' needs.

The Kroger Company

"Our mission is to be a performance-proven leader in the distribution and merchandising of food, health, personal care, and related consumable products and services. In achieving this objective, we will satisfy our responsibilities to shareowners, employees, customers and the communities we serve.

We will conduct our business to produce financial returns that encourage and reward investment by shareowners and allow the company to grow. Investments in retailing, distribution, and processing will be continually evaluated for their contribution to our corporate return objectives.

We will constantly strive to satisfy consumer needs as well as or better than the best of our competitors. Operating procedures will increasingly reflect our belief that the organizational levels closest to the consumer are best positioned to respond to the changing needs of the consumer.

We will treat our employees fairly and with respect, openness and honesty. We will solicit and respond to their ideas and reward meaningful contributions to our success. We will encourage our employees to be active and responsible citizens and will allocate resources for activities which will enhance the quality of life for our customers, employees and the general public."

This mission statement has completely lost focus of its purpose. First of all, it is too long. It contains statements that have no significance. Remember, the purpose of the mission statement is to provide parameters for the organization's strategy. Instead, Kroger has used the mission statement to address the firm's stockholders and their employees. As far as mission statements go, it is totally inappropriate. Other than that, they have clearly indicated what business they are in, which is the distribution and merchandising of food, health, personal care and related consumable products and services. They have not specified who their customers are but instead they seem to serve communities in general, which is a very broad market on which to focus their strategies. The need of their customers seems to be "change." They seem to have completely missed the target with regard to needs. Even though they have not established the specific needs of their customers, they say they hope to strive to be the best. This is a highly irrational and illogical statement because it cannot be measured, therefore it cannot be achieved. We will speak more of this in the next chapter when the topic of goals is discussed.

The mission statements listed below are evaluated in Table 2.1, which indicates if each company has addressed the four questions we have been discussing.

1. Honeywell, Inc.

Honeywell is dedicated to a century-old heritage: helping people control their world. Control technology began with a Honeywell invention. It grew with Honeywell innovations. It remains the core of our business, as we provide control that enables people around the world to live better and work more productively.

2. American Airlines

We will be the global market leader in air transportation and related services. That leadership will be attained by setting the industry standard for safety and security providing world class customer service and consistently superior financial returns for shareholders.

3. Phillips Petroleum Company

Our statement of mission is to enhance the value of our shareholders' investments by using the strengths of our people and our integrated operations to provide our customers with products that are high quality and competitive in price.

4. Whirlpool Corporation

To become the premier company in meeting the durable service needs of Sears' domestic and global customers. To accomplish this, we must be best at what we do, having the highest quality people, products and services, all aimed at continually meeting customer needs on a worldwide basis.

5. Du Pont

Du Pont is a diversified chemical, energy and specialty company with a strong tradition of discovery. Our global businesses are constantly evolving and continually searching for new and better ways to use our human, technological, and financial resources to improve the quality of life of people around the world.

The mission that drives us is ongoing and challenging...to increase the value of the company to customers, employees and shareholders by profitably providing beneficial products and services to worldwide markets. In doing so, each of our businesses must deliver financial results superior to those of its leading competitors.

While much of our growth occurs through discovery and development of new products, our success depends ultimately upon our total commitment to serving the needs of the market place. Above all, we recognize that the degree of our success is in direct proportion to the quality and dedication of our people.

COMPANY	WHO ARE WE	WHO DO WE SERVE	WHAT ARE THEIR NEEDS	HOW DO WE MEET THOSE NEEDS
Honeywell, inc.	-	-	-	-
American Airlines	x	-	x	-
Plillips Petroleum	-	-	-	x
Whirlpool Corp.	x	x	-	-
Du Pont	x	x	x	x

Table 2.1

As shown in Table 2.1, even these well regarded companies do not address the questions which we consider vital. Although, they are not issues that should be overlooked, it does not necessarily mean that they can not be successful. But, responding to the four questions will certainly increase their probability of success since, without answering the questions, these companies are building their whole strategic structure on a shaky foundation.

In summary, each organization has a unique purpose for being. This uniqueness should be reflected in the firm's mission statement. An organization can achieve a heightened sense of purpose when managers and employees develop and communicate a clear business mission. Quoting Drucker, "The first responsibility of a strategist is developing a clear business statement."

A well designed mission statement is essential for developing and implementing a strategic plan. A company cannot run smoothly if its managers and employees do not know what business they are in or who their customers are. Leonardo DaVinci would not have developed the masterpiece of the mysterious Mona Lisa if he had not first decided who his subject was going to be and projected that unique smile.

Goals and Objectives

As painters, now that we have defined the parameters of our painting, we can determine what specifically we need to include in our painting in order that we may present what we wish our audience to perceive. The same is true with strategic planning. This is the second step of the strategic planning process, and is appropriately labeled "goals and objectives".

However, before we can define them, we first have to define what we mean by goals and by objectives. You may think you know the answer, but the real truth is that the definition is different and uncertain, depending to whom you are speaking. I would define goals as short-term in nature and objectives as long-term in nature. For example, you could say that we need to accomplish our goals in order to reach our final objective. However, others may see it differently. Perhaps the best approach is to simply go along with the way your organization defines it because it won't make much of a difference as long as they are on the same track. Just make sure that you are all in agreement. In this book, we will define goals as short term and objectives as long term. For instance, Ford Motor Company's goal would be to increase its market share by 2% until they reach their objective of being the market leader.

Peter Drucker lists seven areas in which he thinks goals should be formulated:

1. Market Standing - the firm should state the market share percentage it seeks.
2. Innovation - the firm should establish targets for new products and services, reduction of costs, financing, performance of operations, and management of human resources and information.
3. Productivity - the firm should set targets for efficient use of resources.
4. Physical and financial resources - The firm should state how it intends to acquire and efficiently use these resources.
5. Profitability - It should establish targets for return to owners as measured by various indices.
6. Manager performance and development - It should define how well managers are expected to perform and how it will measure actual performance. Desired future performance levels should be ensured through development programs and targets.
7. Worker performance and attitude - Specific performance levels should be sought and actual performance measured. Attitude types and levels should also be sought.

Shown on the next page are the results of the 82-company study conducted by Y. K. Shetty. Table 2.2 shows the number of companies having goals in each category. The reason the percentages add up to more than 100% is because most of these companies had more than one goal. This helps us to get an idea of where it might be important to set goals.

CATEGORY	NUMBER	PERCENT
Profitability	73	89
Growth	67	82
Market Share	54	66
Social responsibility	53	65
Employee welfare	51	62
Product quality and service	49	60
Research and development	44	54
Diversification	42	51
Efficiency	41	50
Financial stability	40	49
Resource conservation	32	39
Management development	29	35
Multinational enterprise	24	29
Consolidation	14	17
Miscellaneous goals	15	18

Table 2.2

Criteria for Goals and Objectives

Goals and objectives cannot just be stated in an organization, there are some rules that have to observed for them to be effective:

Measurability and Definability

The most important qualities that a goal or objective must exhibit is that of measurability and definability. If goals can not be measured or defined, what good are they? This does not mean that they have to be quantifiable. You don't necessarily have to say that your goal is to increase sales by $150,000. You could, for example, say that your company needs to be recognized as a trustworthy company. This could be measured by taking a survey and determining if a majority of people perceive your company as trustworthy. It is inappropriate, however, to have a goal or object to be "better" or "the best." What does "better" or "best" mean? It could be different for everyone. It is not uncommon for companies to make these kinds of generalizations. It's a good way for executives to hide their incompetence.

Goals are not restricted to independent values. They can also be values that are functions of other measures. An independent value would be, "I want sales to be two million dollars this year," while a dependent value would be, "I want our profits to increase in the same proportion to the increase of our market share." In other words, we are looking at a proportion of market share increase as a measure of profits. Another example would be Boeing's goal for profitability. For them, "profitability is measured against our ability to achieve and then maintain a 20% average return on stock holders' equity."

Also, you can either have an explicit value as a goal or objective or you can have a range of acceptance values. A firm's goal could be to have 22 million dollars in sales, which is an explicit value, or the firm could state that it wants 22 million dollars in sales, plus or minus 2 million in sales, which means its range is between 20 to 24 million dollars in sales.

Incorporate the Dimension of Time

If goals and objectives are to be useful, they have to say what is going to happen, and when, such as, "our objective is to increase sales from $10 million this year to $50 million five years from now." Goal measurement is usually meaningless without a time frame. For instance, a firm that wants to move up from number six to number two in market share in two years faces a far greater challenge than a similar firm that allows itself 10 years. The Tribune Company has an annual goal to achieve a 20% growth in earnings, 20% return on equity and a 20% return on invested cash.

The goal objective for General Electric when Jack Welsh was the CEO was to, "become a $10 billion company with 10% after-tax profits by the mid-1990's. That is our dream, that is our common vision and that is what we are working toward."

Obtainability

Finally the question always arises as to the degree of obtainability or the probable difficulty of achieving any specific set goals and objectives. For instance, if you set a goal, should it be unobtainable and difficult or obtainable and easy? Some firms set unreachable goals to allow the firm to strive beyond normal constraints in order to achieve heights greater than thought possible. On the other hand, some firms make it easy so that the employees will have the satisfaction of being able to achieve their goals. But research has shown that by making goals and objectives too difficult, people tend to loose interest, resulting in a negative attitude. On the other hand, when goals are too easy to obtain, people tend to take them for granted, thereby reducing efficiency. Which approach do you think is better? The literature supports the idea that it is best to have goals and objectives that are difficult yet obtainable. However, like any rule, there are always exceptions. Perhaps the proper method is to first look at your organization's culture, then decide.

Summary

Like any painter, the manager or entrepreneur in search of a winning strategy must not only have a source, or pallet, of creative options, but also a process or system which allows him or her to effectively and efficiently make the appropriate choice.

For the landscape painter, the first two steps of this process are to set the parameters of the painting as exemplified by defining the horizon, and then to determine, specifically, what he or she wishes to accomplish. For a manager wishing to create a successful strategy, this process is strategic planning, and the first and second steps are mission statement development and then setting the organization's goals and objective.

Effective mission statements are a rarity in today's business world. The fact that their purpose is to define the organization is often overlooked, as they usually are used as propaganda for the organization's stakeholders. Good mission statements must provide answers to four questions: What is our business or who are we? Who are our customers or who do we serve? What are the needs of those we serve? How do we meet these needs?

After the mission statement is developed it is important to set goals and objectives. One problem with this procedure is that people often have a different understanding of what goals and objectives are. After this is clarified, your goals and objectives must have the following attributes: (1) measurability and definability, (2) incorporate the dimension of time, and (3) obtainability.

Chapter 3

Capabilities and Outside Factors: Environmental Scanning

Most painters don't just wake up one day, decide to become painters, and then start to paint. Generally, they have spent many years developing their own skills while reviewing what others have done. In other words, they have an idea of what their capabilities are as a painter and what is available to them that can assist them in presenting their ideas. The same is true when a company starts on the path of success. In business, this process of understanding what our capabilities are and what is going on in the world around us is often called "environmental scanning." Specifically, when we are reviewing our capabilities, we are looking for our strengths and weaknesses. When we are reviewing the external world, we are looking for opportunities and threats. Therefore, environmental scanning is also referred to as a SWOT analysis, SW for strengths and weaknesses, and OT for opportunities and threats.

The question often arises as to the relative importance of our strengths and weakness and opportunities and threats. It can be argued that all are equally important. However, it can also be argued that weaknesses are more important than strengths, and that threats are more important than opportunities. The reason is that if you are not sure of your strengths, the only loss you may suffer is that you do not take complete advantage of an opportunity. On the other hand, if you miss your weaknesses, your company can suffer an irreparable competitive error. The same is true in the external environment. If you miss an opportunity, others may come by. However, if you miss a threat, you may never get another chance to take advantage of an opportunity. Because of this, good strategic planners are often considered to be pessimists. They focus on weaknesses and threats. But they are the ones that ensure the company's survival. People often approach with "great deals" where you "can't lose," but beware of the flipside. There are always weaknesses and threats.

The process of creating successful strategies requires careful analysis of an organization's capabilities as well as a thorough understanding of those forces outside of the organization's control. These forces can affect not only the success of a particular organization within the industry, but also the industry as a whole.

Accordingly, environmental scanning is the third step in the strategic planning process. In order to facilitate an understanding of this step, I have developed the environmental scanning outline exhibited in Figure 3.1. The purpose of this chapter is to provide you with a working understanding of that outline.

Since the environment can be classified into two groups, external and internal, the environmental scanning outline is first divided into two sections. The section concerned with the organization's capabilities, its strengths and weaknesses (SW), is labeled "Internal". The section concerned about those factors outside of the organization where the opportunities and threats (OT) exist is labeled "External".

Capabilities (Strengths and Weaknesses): The Internal Environment

Like Painters, organizations have to know of what they are capable. They have to have a thorough understanding of where their greatest expertise lies and where it is lacking. In addition, as their abilities and external circumstances change, they must be able to constantly change with them.

In today's dynamic competitive environment, this is also true for competitive organizations. In fact, the ability of an organization to change can in itself be the competitive factor that leads the organization to success. Specifically, organizations must have those particular attributes necessary for success in those industries in which it competes. For example, there is no way an automotive company can be successful without good quality control.

In order to facilitate a complete review of an organization's capability to compete, internal environmental scanning should include critiquing the organization's structure, culture and resources.

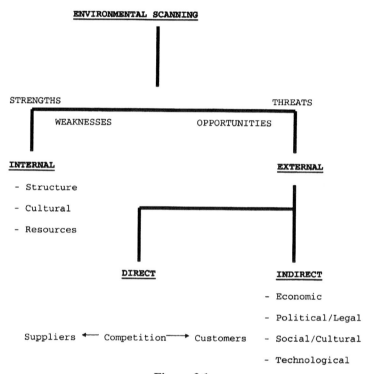

Figure 3.1

Structure

The structure of an organization is often defined in terms of communication, authority and workflow. However it is much more than just the relationship between the people and the roles they play in the company. Structure can be defined as the framework that supports the organization's processes. It could include such things as location and layout of manufacturing and office facilities. Isn't the boss's office usually located on the top floor?

Typically though, organizational hierarchical relationships are the first elements of concern. These relationships are often delineated in chart form. They explicitly show who reports to whom and who has authority over what parts of the organization.

There are many types of hierarchical structural forms, but the four most prominent include simple, functional, divisional, and matrix.

A simple structure (Figure 3.2) is the most basic form of hierarchical structure. A firm with a simple structure is likely to be managed by an owner, who oversees all of the organization's operations. Each employee reports directly to the owner or manager. Because employees have direct access to the final decision-maker, a simple structure allows the organization to be extremely flexible and

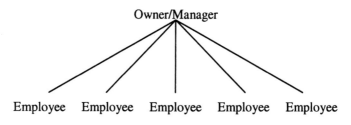

Owner/Manager

Employee   Employee   Employee   Employee   Employee

Simple Structure
Figure 3.2

respond quickly. This ability is especially useful when an organization is new and small, since new organizations often lack the resources of large organizations and are limited in their competitive capabilities. As a result, they must rely on their ability to be flexible and quick responding.

However, the benefit of being able to go right to the top for a decision is usually the very same reason this type of organization structure fails. As the organization grows, more and more decisions have to be made. Since only one person has the authority to make those decisions, the ability to be quick responding and flexible suffers while everyone waits for a decision to be made by the one decision-maker.

To ease the burden on a single decision-maker, organizations often utilize a functional structure (Figure 3.3). In a functional structure, work is divided into subunits on the basis of the organization's functional units, such as manufacturing, finance, sales, etc. This type of structure enables a firm to take advantage of specialists and to deal with complex problems more efficiently. Workers report to their functional supervisors, and these supervisors report to the organization's chief operating officer. The manager or CEO's job now changes from decision-maker to both decision-maker and coordinator. However, it is important to remember that, unless decision making authority is given to the functional area managers, the organization structure may look different than the simple form, but it is not.

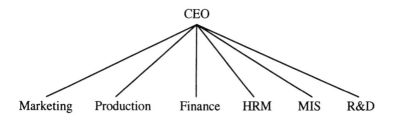

Functional Structure
Figure 3.3

Larger organizations are often strategically divided into units consisting of similar products, product lines, or businesses groups. These units can be labeled divisions, business units, or strategic business units (SBU). This type of structure is called a "divisional structure" (Figure 3.4); it is organized in a way that allows each unit to operate fairly independent of one another. This structure provides the large complex organization the flexibility it needs to operate in multiple dynamic industries.

The matrix structure (Figure 3.5), combines the functional and divisional structures. It does this by employing a matrix format with the vertical axis containing the divisional units or projects, and the horizontal axis containing the different functional areas. With this structure, employees have two superiors, a project manager and a function manager. This type of structure is often used in high-tech industries, where the organization is often working on different

Divisional Structure
Figure 3.4

"projects". This structure allows for the team approach and provides the benefits associated with that type of approach. On the other hand, conflict abounds in this type of structure, as each employee reports to two different managers, the function manager and the project manager, and resources are fought over between the two.

	Marketing	Production	Finance	HRM	MIS	R&D
Proj. 1						
Proj. 2						
Proj. 3						

Matrix Structure
Figure 3.5

It is important to understand that these hierarchical structure forms are not necessarily independent. Organizations can incorporate all of these forms. For example, one business unit of a company may utilize the simple structure, while another business unit of the same company may utilize the functional structure. In addition, a company may have an overall divisional structure, while each of its divisions themselves may be utilizing any one of the other structures.

Along with the hierarchical issues, some other items that should be considered when reviewing an organization's structure include organizational boundary spanning capabilities, internal communication networks and business unit make up.

Culture

A corporation's culture can be defined as the set of expectations, values and norms which are shared by the firm's members. These three segments of culture make up the acceptable behavior from top management to employees. Therefore, culture affects an organization's ability to shift its strategic direction. Some organizations, for example, do not have a culture that allows its strategic direction to change. Its members are unable to cope with the uncertainty that accompanies dynamic situations. Before any strategy is attempted, it is important to know about your organization's culture so this issue can be addressed during implementation. You may have developed a great strategy, but if your organization will not accept it because it runs contrary to the organization's culture, you will not be able to implement it.

An example of how understanding your company's culture can impact your success was Delta Airlines. Part of the culture within Delta was that the company had a good relationship with its their employees. In order for Delta to stay profitable they had to come up with a strategy that would keep them competitive. They decided to look internally to see what could be done to reduce their operation budget. They called their effort Leadership 7.5, relating to their goal of $.75 cents per unit cost. Delta looked at all three of the internal pieces in the environmental scanning outline. They knew that they needed to depend on the honesty and help of their employees. As they had hoped, that paid off with the support of their employees. During the process of planning Leadership 7.5, some of their employees recommended that their own jobs be eliminated. The employees have also appreciated Delta's honesty and advance warning about layoffs. The availability and ultimate success of Delta's strategy was a function of understanding the organization's culture. Let's hope that in today's volatile airline environment, Delta remembers how important understanding an organization's culture can be.

Resources

When one thinks of resources, financial resources generally come to mind. In other words, how much cash do we have on hand, and how much of our potential borrowing power do we still have available. However, there are two other kinds of resources. They include both physical and human.

Physical resources can be classified as plant, property and equipment. "Plant" consists of all of your physical facilities, such as office buildings and factories. "Property" is the land that you both own and rent. "Equipment" includes everything utilized by your organization that allows you to provide your customers with the organization's services and products. Equipment includes such things as desks, chairs, computers (both hardware and software), copying machines, production machinery, transportation equipment (cars, trucks, planes, trains), etc. It also includes the processes that are used when the equipment is operated.

Human resources considers the employees of the organization, looking at both the numbers and individual skills of both management and the labor force.

When conducting an internal environmental scan of your organization, you should first get a handle on the structure, culture and resources of the company as a whole. After that, a closer review of each business unit's physical and human resources is required. Remember, what you are trying to determine is your organization's strengths and weaknesses.

Outside Factors (Opportunities & Threats): The External Environment

Once a painter is knowledgeable and in command of his or her capabilities, he or she must also consider those external factors which may both limit and enhance the ability to achieve full potential. For example, for painters to fully express themselves, they must consider such external factors as the availability of subject matter, lighting, pigments, canvas, and supplies. There may be an instance when, for a short period of time, a hard to find special pigment becomes available. This opportunity must be taken advantage of if they are to express themselves in a bold and expressive manner made possible with only these pigments. On the other hand, when painting a landscape, painters must be aware of the change of seasons. If they are not, they may not have enough time to complete their painting. In other words, the changing seasons can threaten their ability to complete their painting.

The painter also affects the environment in which he or she is working. For example, once a new technique is developed, other painters often try to emulate it.

The same is true with competitive organizations. No company operates in a vacuum. Organizations are considered open systems, which interact with their environment. Like the painter, they must be aware of threats to, and opportunities available to, their companies. And, just like the painter, when reviewing these issues it is important to remember that not only does the external environment affect us, but we affect it.

Different categories of threats and opportunities interact directly and indirectly with organizations. Therefore, an easy way to conduct an external environmental analysis is to review those threats and opportunities that affect the organization directly, and those that affect the organization indirectly.

Indirect environment

When reviewing those environmental factors that are the source of indirect threats and opportunities, you should take into account environmental areas including economic conditions, politics and legal concerns, social and cultural issues, demographics, and technological issues.

Economic Conditions

Of the four indirect environmental factors mentioned above, it is the economic environment that usually has the most dramatic effect on business. It is well documented that a nation's economic state influences the strategies and performance of a company. Some of the most prominent indicators of economic growth or stagnation are Gross National Product (GNP), inflation rates, stock market growth rates, money supply, balance of trade, and balance of payments. However, some indicators have even more impact. They include interest rates, international exchange rates, labor supply, and a myriad of specific indicators such as inventory levels and housing start-ups. Most of the economic indicators that are important to a particular organization would depend upon the territory it serves, the kind of customer or client, and the product or service it provides.

In today's global economic environment, each nation's economy is linked to other nations around the world. Therefore, a competing organization has to consider not only those economic factors which affect it at home, but also the economic conditions in foreign countries where it is presently conducting operations and where it may eventually be operating.

Businesses need to consider the state of a nation's domestic economy because it is a good indicator of that country's economic stability. What, for example, is the ability of a country to pay its debts, or are there cash exchange restrictions?

The above represent only a few of the economic considerations with which a company has to be concerned. This area has become important enough that several organizations, such as the World Bank and private specialized companies, prepare regular analysis of each country's domestic environment, including global implications.

Political/Legal

Political and legal developments can expand or limit a company's freedom of action and make the environment more hostile or more supportive of its activities. Political and legal changes are easier to identify than social changes, but are often harder to interpret than demographic indicators. The body of government and professional regulations that affect the operations of an organization and the record and attributes of political parties certainly need to be tracked.

The nature and likelihood of new, emerging and changing regulations of strategic significance are of great importance. The deregulation of industries such as airlines, telecommunications, and banking has resulted in revolutionary changes. Environmental regulations, even apparently minor developments such as banning of cyclamates, have proven to be traumatic to particular industries. Federal regulations have changed the nature of the workplace and the basic economics of many industries. They have even been the harbinger of entirely new industries.

As with economic issues, the advent of a global marketplace brings additional concerns when analyzing the political and legal environments. In addition to the politics and legal regulations of their home country, organizations now have to be concerned with these issues in countries where they have operations.

Also, in today's highly dynamic political environment, the issue of political stability comes into play. An organization may have agreements with a government that may or may not be in power tomorrow.

Social/Cultural

Social attitudes and cultural values can have a significant impact on a business. For example, in the U.S., there has been an increase of women in the workforce since 1970. A significant number of women between twenty and fifty years of age work outside of the home. As a result, disposable income has increased, thus increasing the demand for items such as cars, homes and leisure travel.

Social and cultural changes can pose a threat to businesses. In the U.S., millions of adults lack basic reading, writing and math skills. Consequently, in order to be competitive, more than half of the Fortune 500 companies have had to assume an important role in educating the workforce.

Demographic issues are also of great concern to any organization providing a product or service to the populace. It seems that in today's world, population attributes are changing faster than ever. When you consider the entire world, this is even more true. Populations are constantly shifting and changing their characteristics.

The most significant international demographic factor is the shear increase in population, especially in the developing nations. The world's population doubled in the decade of the 1990's. Still, some countries have not yet even started to realize the consequences of such growth. Basic issues such as food and water are now becoming important concerns. Illegal aliens are posing a threat to the United States, while other countries face the problem of unconstrained immigration. However, good planners have been turning these "threats' into opportunities, as this increase in population opens new and exciting markets.

Technological

When we speak about technology in the indirect external environment, we are not talking about the technology that is prevalent in an industry. This investigation occurs when we are looking at the competition,   which is discussed in the next section, "Direct Environment." Technology in the indirect environment refers to the technology available to the society surrounding our organization.

One way technology in the indirect environment affects an organization is through the technological capacity of the society where it markets its products. There is no sense in selling computers in third world countries where there is hardly any communication infrastructure.

But simply knowing the level of technology in the countries where the organization operates is not enough. The rate of change of those technologies is also important.   Questions must be asked regarding how long the current state of a society's technology will stay in place before it becomes obsolete and how adaptable to technological change that society is.

Direct Environment

There are many possible topics that could be included when discussing the direct environment. Because there are so many topics, many categorization schemes and analytical approaches to review them have been suggested. However, almost all include the key areas of suppliers, competition, and customers

Suppliers

Suppliers can, and often do, have great impact on the success or failure of a business.   Over the years the relationship between companies and their suppliers has changed dramatically. At one time the companies ruled the roost. They had many suppliers and often played them against one another.   This drove the price of supplies down dramatically.

Historically, the relationship between suppliers and customers was based upon three factors: price, quality, and delivery. In other words, could customers get a product at a low price, with high quality, and delivered when they needed it? Generaly they had to settle for two of the three. If they could get a low price, and high quality, then they would have to wait for delivery. On the other hand, if they wanted a high quality product delivered when they needed it, they usually had to pay a higher price.

However, with the advent of computer applications, companies can work closely with just a few suppliers. Often, their systems are so connected that deliveries are made only when materials are needed, as with JIT delivery systems. The development of e-business applications has brought an even closer relationship between supplier and company. Today, companies can now provide low price, high quality, and JIT delivery.

Competitors

It is very important to understand your competition. Accordingly, much has been written on this topic, however, you can have an advantage. If you look at the elements of the internal analysis in the environmental scanning outline you will have an idea of what kind of information is needed about the competition. You need to know the same things about your competition that you know about your own company. You need to know each competitor's structure, culture, and especially resources (human, physical, and financial). Remember that it is important to know not only what resources they have, but how they are using those resources. For example, what are they doing with their production facilities to make them more competitive? How are they utilizing their marketing resources to promote and sell their products? These are the types of important questions to which you must find answers.

In addition to the particular questions regarding individual competitors, it is also important to understand the implications of the degree of competitive intensity. For example, is this industry in high growth, or is it in maturity or decline, where competitive intensity is not so great? Are there a lot of competitors or few? Can anyone easily enter the industry? All of these questions and others relating to the industry as a whole must be answered.

Customers

Companies are in business to meet customers' needs with products and services. Understanding your customers and clients is an integral and important part of business. One entire business function is devoted to the mission of customer relations; it's called marketing. All those things that you have come to know about marketing fall into this part of the environmental scanning outline. As with the competitor analysis, customer/client information can be put into two areas, one concerning the individual, and the other concerning all of the customers and clients as a group.

When looking at the individual, issues such as who these people or organizations are, and what their needs are become important. When looking at the group, issues relating to the size, growth and potential are important.

Environmental Forecasting

Now that all of the information about both the external and internal environments is gathered, you would think that it was time to develop strategies. But the reality is that you have a problem to solve before you can begin. The problem lies in the fact that the information you have gathered is for yesterday and today, and the strategy you are developing is for tomorrow. So, you have to utilize some method which will allow you to take this historical and current data and develop it into information about the internal and external environment of tomorrow.

Of the two, internal and external, internal is fairly easy since it consists of those things which are controllable. We can make our organization into what we want it to be. However, the same is not true about the external environment because it contains factors that are uncontrollable. Those processes that are designed specifically to provide inferences about the future are called forecasting techniques.

The role of forecasting in strategic management is to reduce uncertainty and support decision-making. This task is made even more difficult in today's highly dynamic environment. One or more years frequently elapse between the conception and implementation of a new strategy. During this time, the assumptions or premises on which the strategy and its implementation was based may change significantly. Rapid change is compressing these time horizons.

No one can deny that economical, technological, political and social change is part of organizational life. Given that fact, the obvious question is, how can these changes be forecasted? To say the least, forecasting is a most difficult process. At this point it may be consoling to recall some humorous forecasting sayings:

1. It is very difficult to forecast especially the future.
2. Those who live by the crystal ball soon learn to eat ground glass.

3. The moment you forecast, you know that you are going to be wrong. You just can't know the future.
4. Don't spend a lot on a forecaster. He or she can't predict the future anymore than you can.

Regardless of the strong possibility of error, to be successful, organizations must forecast their future environment. Several studies have examined the impact of environmental analysis and forecasting on organizational performance. One study found that increased knowledge through environmental analysis and forecasting was positively correlated to profitability. Furthermore, a study of 21 companies in the United Kingdom found that the companies that gathered and used more environmental information had a higher financial performance than those that used less information.

Some of the most common methods used for forecasting are trend-impact analysis, statistical analysis, and scenarios.

Trend-Impact Analysis

Trend-impact analysis is one method used in environmental forecasting. It is conducted through the following general steps.

> *Step 1*: Past history of a particular phenomenon is extrapolated with the help of a computer.
> *Step 2*: A panel of experts specifies a set of unique future events that could have a bearing on the phenomenon under study.
> *Step 3*: A panel of experts indicates how the trend extrapolation would be affected by the occurrence of each of these events.
> *Step 4*: A computer then modifies that trend extrapolation by using these judgements.
> *Step 5*: A panel of experts reviews the adjusted extrapolation and modifies the inputs.

Statistical Analysis

Another forecasting technique is statistical analysis. Statistical analysis is a quantitative technique that attempts to discover causal, or at the least, explanatory factors that link two or more time series factors together. A popular statistical analytical tool is regression analysis.

The problem with these forecasting methods is that they generally do not take into account events that have never happened before. They are most often based on historical data. Another problem lies in the time span utilized, in that results can be affected by the time frame used when collecting data.

Scenario Forecasting

Today, in order to counteract the problems associated with historical-data-based-forecasting methods, scenario forecasting is most often used. Scenario forecasting involves bringing in experts in each of the different categories of environmental scanning and getting their opinions on what the environment will be like in the future. They use many techniques to forecast, but one of the most popular is the Delphi technique.

The Delphi technique can perhaps best be understood by examining the steps outlined below.

> *Step 1*: Experts on the subject being forecasted are used.
> *Step 2*: The experts are kept apart and anonymous from one another and asked for their forecast on the subject under study. The experts give their answers in a letter to a coordination forecaster.
> *Step 3*: The coordinator determines the consensus of opinion of individual forecasts. Another questionnaire is then sent to the experts giving what the consensus opinion was and asks if they would like to change their opinions in light of the results. This step is repeated until the experts stop changing their opinions. When this happens, the final consensus opinion of the experts is used as the basis for the scenario.

Scenarios are written as if tomorrow is today. It is important to do this because we are going to formulate a strategy that fits into that environment. We therefore have to take our best shot at the future.

I get the strongest arguments from business people who want to know what sense it is to develop strategies based on a definitive and explicit future when there is very little possibility that the future can be predicted. My answer to them is "What is the alternative?" In the best case scenario, if we predicted the future correctly, we could then develop a good strategy that would fit perfectly with that scenario, implement it, and then we would be in a great position to be competitive. In the worst case situation, we would not develop strategies because we felt that there was no way to predict the future, leaving us vulnerable to the market and competition. What we then would have had to do was wait until we saw what was happening, respond to what was happening externally, and then try to make an immediate change. Making rapid, immediate, and complete change is very difficult and often expensive. Failure is the most common result.

What happens if we build a strategy based on an expected future, and that future turns out not to be what we predicted? Let say, for example, that what we predicted was only half correct. Now, our organization only has to make some changes, as we had prepared for some of those changes that did occur. Also, it is much easier to implement these changes over a period of time than to wait to the last minute and try to immediately change. So, even though we do not know for sure what the future is, it is probably a much better idea to at least have a guesstimate about what the future holds and start down the path of strategy implementation. In addition, we have a strategic planning system that allows us to monitor the environment and make corrective modifications if and when those unforecasted changes occur. This surely is a much better approach than going into the future blindfolded.

It should also be obvious that the better we predict, the better off we are, because it means we have to make fewer changes. So it behooves us to take whatever steps are necessary to predict what the conditions are going to be in those areas that we have defined as relevant in the external environment.

Don't be concerned if you cannot reach perfection. Just do your best. There is no book out there that I know of that tells what the interest rate will be five years from now. What you do is paint a scenario of the future.

There are two different approaches involving the inclusion of information in a scenario. One is to paint a general scenario that covers everything relating all the elements in the external environment. This is a massive amount of information that will cost a lot of money and take time to go through. But, it covers everything, leaving out nothing that we might not have otherwise considered.

The alternative is an industry specific scenario. Do not confuse industry specific with company specific. For example, Coca-Cola would look at information relating to all of the beverage industry, not only the information relating to Coke. Remember, the company's mission statement helps define what industry it is in. The advantage of an industry specific scenario is that the data is manageable. There is a saying that too much information is worse than none at all. The disadvantage is that an industry specific scenario might exclude some information that is felt to be unimportant, when in fact, it really is.

With the forecasted data in hand, we can now move forward and start to paint some successful strategies.

Summary

Before we can really start to paint it is probably a good idea to get an understanding of what our capabilities are as a painter, and what is available to us that can help us present our ideas. In business, this is called environmental scanning. Environmental scanning considers both internal and external environments. When looking internally, we are trying to determine our strengths and weaknesses. When looking externally, we are trying to determine any opportunities for, or threats to, our company. Because of the complexity of the issue, an outline is developed (Figure 3.1) which presents the different areas that need to be explored. Internally we look at structure, culture, and resources.

The external environment is divided into two distinct areas. They included the direct external environment, and the indirect external environment. The direct external environment consists of suppliers, competition, and customers. These are things that affect us directly and that we affect directly. The indirect external environment consists of economic considerations, political/legal considerations, social/cultural considerations, and the technological level of the society where we are conducting operations.

Once the information is gathered, a problem arises since the data represents information that is both historical and of the present, and the strategies we are developing will not be fully operational until sometime in the future. The question then is how to project the data into the future.

To accomplish this, three kinds of forecasting techniques are used. They include trend-impact analysis, statistical analysis, and scenario forecasting. Of these, scenario forecasting is the method most often used.

Chapter 4

Sketching: Financial Modeling

The parameters of our strategy have been set, our goals have been defined in specific terms, and information about our organization and its external environment has been gathered and projected into the future. The problem of developing strategy can now be approached. Before some creative strategic approaches can be developed, the optional allocation of resources between the organization's products, product lines, or business units needs to occur to assure that a proper foundation is in place that can support the development of a strong competitive position.

The strategic options outline provides for two alternate strategic groupings. One is allocation strategies and the other is competitive strategies. The allocation side is further divided into financial and portfolio models. Both are used to help allocate human, financial, and physical resources.

Financial models are often used to help financial institutions develop a "balanced" portfolio, thereby increasing overall long-term performance. Likewise, they can also be used to analyze and allocate resources to a company's products, product lines or business units, serving as the foundation that is used to develop ideas.

Painters first develop a rough sketch of what they are going to paint. After this sketch is complete, they then have a clearer picture of what they need to do to achieve their objectives. This approach also works for financial planners. One can equate the sketching to financial modeling.

Financial data is rather straightforward and can be used to quickly paint an outline of the company. This outline can then be used as the basis for a creative competitive strategy.

The strategic palette options outline divides financial models into two categories. They include "simple financial models" and "complex financial models." The majority of this chapter is devoted to explaining what these are and how they are used. There are literally hundreds of financial models, often being developed by consulting firms so they can use them to acquire new clients. Many complex financial models are tied directly to stock performance. Because there are so many models and because many are very complex, we will discuss only a few of them, placing emphasis on the simple financial models. However, don't let the term "simple" confuse you. They may be referred to as simple, yet they are very powerful.

Simple Financial Models

Almost every company uses simple financial models to assess their overall situation and to pinpoint any problem areas. Simple financial models can be raw financial data such as income and loses or cash generated as illustrated in the company's financial statements, or they can be financial ratios computed from that data.

When analyzing simple financial models utilizing both financial statements and financial ratios it is important to conduct both time-series analysis (trend analysis) and a present status analysis. Both of these analyses should be done (1) between your company's products, product lines and/or business units themselves and (2) between each product, product line and/or business unit's performance as compared to the industry norms and/or the best performers in the industry.

Time-series analysis (trend analysis) is merely looking at the financial data over different intervals of time. Although this information can be valuable, if used by itself, it can be very misleading. For example, you might discover that revenues have been declining in a particular business unit over the past few years. This would initially lead you to believe that the existing strategy was not working very well. However, if you compare the percent decline to the industry, making sure that you use the same time interval, you might find that everyone else is doing much worse. The industry is in fact declining at a much greater rate than your business unit is. From this you could assume that your strategy might be just fine, but the industry as a whole is not doing well. Your strategic choices would be quite different. Present status analysis takes a snapshot of where your organization is right now.

Financial Statement Analysis

The two primary financial statements used to analyze a company and its SBU's are the balance sheet and the income statement. Examples of a balance sheet and an income statement are presented in Figure 4.1 and Figure 4.2.

Reviewing the balance sheet, we first can see that our example company is using up its cash. Whether or not it has an appropriate amount of cash is determined first by comparing the example company's cash position to that of the competition, and then by checking through the use of financial ratios, which will later be discussed. However, a 48.9 percent drop in cash is significant. The company appears to be doing better in collecting its receivables since receivables have decreased by 50 percent. Also, the company's inventory has gone down significantly as well. This may be an indication that the company is getting better control over its inventory or it may mean that production is not able to produce enough product. But it appears that this is an issue that needs to be checked into. These are a few of the items of interest that can help in understanding how the company is performing both in the past and the present. All of the other areas of the balance sheet should also be compared to industry norms.

The first item on the income statement is sales. Our example company's sales have increased by 8.3 percent over a one year period. Initially this indicates that Example Company is doing a better job at selling its products. However, this percentage should really be compared to the market growth rate and the growth rate of the leading competitors before any conclusions can be drawn.

Cost of goods sold has increased as expected, but at a rate greater than that of sales. Is Example Company operating less efficiently? Gross margins have actually gone down.

Although selling expenses have gone up, they appear to be in line with the increase of sales. For the $500,000 increase in sales, the company received $4,000,000 in revenues.

EXAMPLE COMPANY
Comparative Balance Sheet
December 31, 1998, and 1997
(dollars in thousands)

	1998	1997	Increase (Decrease) Amount	Percent
Assets				
Current assets				
Cash	$1,200	$2,350	$(1,150)	(48.9)
Accounts receivable	6,000	4,000	2,000	50.0
Inventory	8,000	10,000	(2,000)	(20.0)
Prepaid expenses	300	120	180	150.0
Total current assets	15,500	16,470	(970)	(5.9)
Property and equipment				
Land	4,000	4,000	-0-	-0-
Buildings & equipment	12,000	8,500	3,500	41.2
Total property & equip.	16,000	12,500	3,500	28.0
Total assets	$ 31,500	$ 28,970	$ 2,530	8.7
	=====	=====	=====	====
Liabilities & Stockholders' Equity				
Current liabilities				
Accounts payable	$5,800	$4,000	$1,800	45.0
Accrued payables	900	400	500	125.0
Notes payable (short term)	300	600	(300)	(50.0)
Total current liabilities	7,000	5,000	2,000	40.0
Long-term liabilities				
Bonds payable (8%)	7,500	8,000	(500)	(6.3)
Total liabilities	14,500	13,000	1,500	11.5
Stockholders' equity				
Preferred stock, $100 par, 6%,				
$100 liquidation value	2,000	2,000	-0-	-0-
Common stock $12 par	6,000	6,000	-0-	-0-
Additional paid in capital	1,000	1,000	-0-	-0-
Total paid in capital	9,000	9,000	-0-	-0-
Retained earnings	8,000	6,970	1,030	14.8
Total stockholders equity	17,000	15,970	1,030	6.4
Total				
Liabilities & stockholders equity	$31,500	$28,970	$2,530	8.7

Example Balance Sheet
Figure 4.1

EXAMPLE COMPANY
Comparative Income Statement
For the Years Ended December 31, 1998 and 1997
(dollars in thousands)

	1998	1997	Increase (Decrease) Amount	Percent
Sales	$52,000	$48,000	$4,000	8.3
Cost of goods sold	36,000	31,500	4,500	14.3
Gross margin	16,000	16,500	(500)	(3.0)
Operating expenses				
Selling expenses	7,000	6,500	500	7.7
Administration expenses	5,860	6,100	(240)	(3.9)
Total operating expenses	12,860	12,600	260	2.1
Net operating income	3,140	3,900	(760)	(19.5)
Interest expense	640	700	(60)	(8.6)
Net income before taxes	2,500	3,200	(700)	(21.9)
Less income taxes (30%)	750	960	(210)	(21.9)
Net income	1,750	2,240	(490)	(21.9)
Dividends to preferred stockholders, $6 per share	120	120		
Net income remaining for common Stockholders	1,630	2,120		
Dividends to common stockholders, $1.20 per share	600	600		
Net income added to retained earnings	1,030	1,520		
Retained earnings, beginning of year	6,970	5,450		
Retained earnings, end of year	$8,000	$6,970		

Example Income Statement
Figure 4.2

We have only looked at a few of the possible items presented on income statements and balance sheets that can provide valuable information to the strategic planner wishing to optimally allocate their company's resources between its SBU's, and learn specifically where within each SBU those resources should be placed. An initial cursory review of Example Company's financial statements indicates that they are earning a profit, but profits are declining. Further investigation into the company's operations is necessary.

Ratio Analysis

In addition to raw financial data, there are many types of financial ratios that can be used for our analysis. These ratios can be placed into four groups. They include:

1. Liquidity ratios
2. Leverage ratios
3. Profitability ratios
4. Activity ratios

The first two of these, liquidity and leverage ratios, are usually concerned with determining how solvent the company is. In other words, how much cash does the company have and how much can it get. However, they can and often are important performance indicators. Issues of liquidity and leverage are always determined at the "corporate" level, since the liquidity of the company is the same as the liquidity of a business unit. Accordingly, data utilized for these ratios should come from the organization's consolidated statements. If a company has little cash, then each business unit has little cash. On the other hand, profitability and activity ratios, the second two groups of ratios, generally measure performance. Since our analysis of performance takes place at the business unit level, data for these ratios must come from each individual business unit, and then be summarized for overall organization performance.

Liquidity Ratios

These ratios measure the company's ability to meet its financial obligations. The three most important liquidity ratios are the current ratio, quick ratio, and the cash ratio.

Current Ratio

A short term indicator of the company's ability to pay its short-term liabilities from short-term assets. If we put it in another way, it is how much of current assets are available to cover each dollar of current liabilities. The current ratio can be calculated in the following way:

Current assets

Current liabilities

		1998	1997
Current assets	=	15,500,000	16,470,000
Current liabilities	=	7,000,000	5,000,000
Current ratio	=	2.21	3.29

The current ratio must be interpreted with great care. A declining ratio, as above, might be a sign of a deteriorating financial condition. On the other hand, it might be the result of a paring of obsolete inventories or other stagnant current assets. An improving ratio might be the result of an unwise stockpiling of inventory, or it might indicate an improving financial situation. In short, the current ratio is useful but tricky to interpret. To avoid a mistake, the analyst must look hard at the individual assets and liabilities involved.

Generally, a current ratio of 2.0 is occasionally cited as acceptable. But, the more predictable a company's cash flows, the lower the acceptable current ratio. If a company has a current ratio of 1.0, its net working capital is zero. If a company has a current ratio of less than 1.0, it will have negative net working capital.

Quick Ratio (Acid Test)

This measures the company's ability to pay off its short-term obligations from current assets, excluding inventories.

(Current Assets - Inventory)

Current Liabilities

		1998	1997
Current assets	=	15,500,000	16,470,000
Current liabilities	=	7,000,000	5,000,000
Inventory	=	8,000,000	10,000,000
Quick ratio	=	1.1 Rounded	1.3 Rounded

A quick ratio of 1.0 is generally acceptable, but acceptability is influenced by the industry norms. A value of less than 1.0 indicates a dependency on inventory or other current assets to liquidate short-term debt. An inquiry into the reasons for the abundance of inventory is probably a good thing to consider.

These two ratios measure a firm's ability to meet its current liabilities with its current assets. The greater the amount of current assets relative to current liabilities, the safer the firm will be. In the quick ratio, in some cases it is not easy to convert inventory to cash because some of the inventory may be obsolete, or may not even exist.

Cash Ratio

This measures the extent to which the company's capital is in cash or cash equivalents; it shows how much of the current obligations can be paid from cash or near cash assets.

$$\frac{\text{Cash} + \text{Cash equivalents}}{\text{Current liabilities}}$$

Leverage Ratios

The leverage ratios measure the contributions of owners' financing compared with creditors' financing. There are six types of leverage ratios: debt to asset ratio, debt to equity ratio, long-term debt to capital structure, current liabilities to equity ratio, times interest earned, and coverage of fixed charges.

Debt to Asset Ratio

This measures the extent to which borrowed funds have been used to finance the company's assets.

$$\frac{\text{Total debt}}{\text{Total assets}}$$

Debt to Equity Ratio

This measures the funds provided by creditors versus funds provided by owners.

Total debt

Stockholders equity

		1998	1997
Total debt	=	14,500,000	13,000,000
Stockholders equity	=	17,000,000	15,970,000
Quick ratio	=	0.85 to 1	0.81 to 1

Creditors normally like the debt-to-equity ratio to be relatively low. The lower the ratio, the greater the amount of assets being provided by the owners of the company and the greater the protection to the creditors. However, common stockholders would like the ratio to be relatively high. In most industries there are norms as to the right amount of debt to include in the capital structure.

Long Term Debt to Capital Structure

Measures the long-term component of capital structure.

Long term debt

Stockholders equity

Current Liabilities to Equity

Measures the short term financing portion versus that provided by owners.

Current liabilities

Stockholders equity

(The above four are expressed in percentage form)

Times Interest Earned

This indicates the ability of the company to meet its annual interest cost.

(Earnings before taxes + Interest charges)

Interest expense

Earnings before interest
and Income taxes   =   3,140,000
Interest expense   =   640,000
Times interest earned   =   4.9 times

Generally, earnings are viewed as adequate to protect long-term creditors if the times interest earned ratio is 2.0 or more. However, the long-run trend of earnings is important to see how vulnerable the firm is to cyclical changes in the economy.

Coverage of Fixed Charges

This gives a measure of the company's ability to meet all of its fixed charge obligations.

Profit before taxes + Interest charges + Lease charges

Interest charges + Lease obligations

(The above two are expressed in decimal form)

Profitability Ratios

The first of the two types of performance ratios are profitability ratios. They measure the degree of the business unit's success in achieving desired profit levels. The following are five of the most common profitability ratios.

Net Profit Margin

The net profit margin reveals how much profit a firm earns on each dollar of sales. This is not too meaningful because it varies so widely by firm and by industry. To interpret this measure, the manager has to know the trend of the measure over time for a given company or the industry.

Net profit after taxes

Net sales

Gross Profit Margin

This indicates the total margin available to cover other expenses beyond cost of goods sold, and still yield a profit.

Sales – (cost of goods sold)

Net sales

Return on Investment (ROI)

This measures the rate of return on the total assets utilized in the company. A measure of management's efficiency, it shows the return on all the assets under its control regardless of source of financing.

Net profit after taxes

Total assets

Return on Equity

This measures the rate of return on the book value of stock holders total investment in the company.

Net profit after taxes

Stockholders equity

Earnings per Share

This shows the after tax earnings generated for each share of common stock.

Net profit after taxes - Preferred stock dividends

              Average number of common shares

Net profit after taxes	=	1,750,000
Preferred stock dividends	=	120,000
Common shares	=	500,000
EPS	=	$3.26

Activity Ratios

The second types of performance ratios are activity ratios. Activity ratios measure the effectiveness of the corporation's use of resources. There are nine common types of activity ratios.

Inventory Turnover

This measures the number of times that the average inventory of finished goods was turned over or sold during a period of time, usually a year. It is important to note that inventory turnover is defined in terms of the annual cost of goods sold and not in terms of annual sales. Since the inventory account is carried at cost, it must be compared against another cost.

Cost of goods sold

Avg. inventory balance

Cost of goods sold	=	36,000,000
Average inventory balance	=	9,000,000
Inventory turnover	=	4 times

Net Working Capital Turnover

Measures how effectively net working capital is used to generate sales.

Net sales

Net working capital

Asset Turnover

Measures the utilization of all the company's assets. The asset turnover shows how many sales dollars are generated by each dollar of assets. It therefore measures how productively the firm uses its assets.

Sales

Total assets

Fixed Asset Turnover

Measures the utilization of the company's fixed assets (i.e., plant and equipment). It shows how many sales are generated by each dollar of fixed assets.

Sales

Fixed assets

Accounts Receivable Turnover

Indicates the number of times that the accounts receivable are cycled during the period (usually a year).

Annual credit sales

Accounts receivables

Days of Inventory

Measures the number of one day's worth of inventory that a company has on hand at any given time.

$$\frac{\text{Inventory}}{(\text{Cost of goods sold}/365)}$$

Average Collection Period

Indicates the average length of time in days that a company must wait to collect after a sale; it may be compared to the credit terms offered by the company to its customers.

$$\frac{\text{Accounts receivable}}{(\text{Sales for year}/365)}$$

Accounts Payable Period

Indicates the average length of time in days that the company takes to pay its credit purchases.

$$\frac{\text{Accounts payable}}{\text{Purchases for year}/365)}$$

Days of Cash

Indicates the number of days of cash on hand, at present sales levels.

$$\frac{\text{Cash}}{(\text{Net sales for year} / 365)}$$

One thing we see in the above four ratios is that all four ratios use the current assets and the current liabilities. When liquidating assets, what matters is how quickly it can be done. The current assets are made up of mainly cash, accounts receivable, and inventories. Therefore, when liquidating, you should get an account of these figures.

Although inventories come under the current assets section, to get a finer answer on the current assets we have excluded the inventories. Again, in the cash ratio we can see the importance placed on current assets (cash) to meet the corporation's financial obligations.

The second set of ratios stress the importance on profits after taxes, the total margin available to cover expenses, the rate of return on the total assets utilized, and earnings generated for each share of common stock.

Complex Financial Models

In an attempt to correct the narrow perspective of simple financial models, complex financial models take into account a multitude of information, such as the risk of the investment, when the return from the investment will be received, and often some external financial information like stock market performance. These numbers are plugged into a formula to give you a single number, which you can use to compare one investment to another.

Discounted Cash Flow Analysis

Often the value of an investment is derived from the anticipated cash flows. Because these cash flows occur over a period of time, their value is a function of the time period over which they occur. Cash that you receive today is worth more than cash that you will receive sometime in the future. Therefore the "time value" of money needs to be considered when comparing the future stream of cash flows to the current investment outlay. This method most commonly used for assigning the proper time value to money when determining the value of investing in a particular investment (SBU), or even a specific strategy over another investment or strategy is the discounted cash flow (DCF) method.

For example, let's assume that you are thinking of implementing a strategy for one of your SBUs. That strategy will cost your company $100,000 today. However, that strategy will return $8,000 over the next five years. At first this may seem like a good choice since the company will be earning $40,000. However, the company has tied up $100,000 for five years, and perhaps there is another strategic investment within the SBU, or within another SBU, that would yield even more.

That is where the company's "cost of capital" comes in. If there were another strategy for the SBU or another strategy for another SBU that would yield even more, or pay off sooner, then the choice would not be such a good one. The cost of capital represents the company's opportunity cost of giving up one strategy investment for another. Thus it is the minimum return they require to compensate them for giving up the use of the money temporarily.

However, when comparing opportunities, the company's planners shouldn't just focus on the expected yield. Since these returns are only projected returns, they must also take into account the relative riskyness of each project. If one strategy returns 15% and another returns 20%, but the 15% strategy has a 95% probability that it will be successful, and the 20% strategy has only a 25% probability of success, then the smaller returning strategy (15%) is probably the better choice to make.

The Capital Asset Pricing Model (CAPM)

One of the most basic complex financial models is the Capital Asset Pricing Model. Otherwise known as the CAPM, it's a method of assessing the required rate of return of an investment considering the amount of risk involved. In equilibrium, a security is expected to yield a return commensurate to its unavoidable or systematic risk. The general rule is the greater the unavoidable risk of a security, the greater the return expected by the investor from the security. The relationship between expected return, unavoidable risk and the value of securities in this context is the essence of the Capital Asset Pricing Model.

The required rate of return (R) is equal to the risk free rate (Rfr), plus a risk premium (Rp), or $R = Rrf + Rp$. For our purposes, the risk free rate (Rfr) is the same as the current T-Bill rate. It is important to assess your risk premium. If you rearrange the above formula, you can calculate the risk premium, $Rp = R - Rrf$. What this formula infers is that the risk premium (Rp) is equal to the required rate of return less the risk free rate. For example, your required rate of return in 12% and T-Bills are paying 5.5%. Your risk premium is 6.5%

The formula for the CAPM goes beyond finding the risk premium for an individual investment. CAPM assesses the rate of return for a market portfolio. For example, the required rate of return for the market portfolio (Rm) is 10%, and T-Bills (Rf) are paying 5.5%. The market risk premium (Rmp) will be 4.5%. This market risk premium now becomes the standard to which all other investments are measured. Particular investments are looked at to see if they have more or less risk premium than the general market. This standard is otherwise known as Beta. The market Beta is equal to one. If the Beta of your investment is less than one, the risk is less than the market. If the Beta of your investment is more than one, the risk is greater than the market.

In this market, if your SBU were offering a risk premium of 9%, you would expect this SBU to have a Beta of 2.0. This SBU offers twice the premium of the market, but at twice the risk. Remember the general rule that one would want to be compensated with higher premiums when the risk is higher, and will expect lower returns when the risk is lower.

Utilizing the CAPM at the company level with different SBU's is a little more complicated, but would still work, the basic difference being that each SBU would have to be considered as if it were its own company.

Present Value

Once you have determined the cost of capital, you can then compute the present value of the future cash flows and pare that to the size of the investment. This is done by discounting each future payment to its present value at the cost of capital. This also includes the value of the investment at the end of the discounting time period.

The process can be illustrated using our discounted cash flow example. The cash flows are assumed to occur at the end of each year, while the investment occurs at the beginning of the first year when we implement our strategy. The actual DCF computations are shown in Figure 4.3. These computations assume that the risk-free interest rate is 7% and the risk premium is 3%, resulting in a cost of capital of 10%.

Initial Investment $100   Capital cost: 10%

	YEAR 1	YEAR 2	YEAR 3	YEAR 4	YEAR 5
Cash flows	8	8	8	8	8
Ending value					100
Total cash flows	8	8	8	8	108
Discount factor	0.909	0.826	0.751	0.683	0.621
Present values	7.27	6.61	6.01	5.46	67.06

DCF RESULTS:

Total present value	$92.42	(Sum of PVs of year 1-5 cash flows)
Net present value	$7.58	(Total present value-initial investment)

Discounted Cash Flow Calculations
Fig. 4.3

When the expected cash flows, including the return of the initial investment, are discounted at the end of the five years, their total present value ($92,000) is less than the initial investment. The most common value computed in DCF analysis is the net present value (NPV) of an investment. This is simply the difference between the present value of the future net cash flows and the initial investment. A positive NPV indicates that the investment will more than pay for itself, while a negative value means that the investment is not worthwhile, compared to alternative uses of the company's money.

There are many other financial techniques or models that can be used to help allocate a company's resources. Those mentioned the most often include the Internal Rate of Return (IRR); the Q ratio, developed in the early sixties by Nobel-Prize-winning economist, James Tobin; Alfred Rappaport's VROI ratio; and others developed by different consulting firms. Each is fairly complicated and, because each has both strong and weak points, needs to be understood thoroughly before being utilized. There are many good financial texts available that will allow you to develop an understanding of these models.

The biggest advantage to complex financial models is that there seems to be a strong connection between them and stockmarket performance, making it possible to determine the value created from a particular strategy.

The biggest drawback, however, is that they are often only referred to in the context of stock selection and not for resource allocation decisions by the strategic planner. But, if you thoroughly understand them, you should be able to bridge the gap between selecting stocks and selecting SBUs in which to invest.

Summary

Financial models help you, the painter, take your first pass at developing your ideas by increasing the probability for success.

Financial models can be divided into two types, simple and

complex. Simple financial models consist of raw financial data, such as profits or losses, and other combinations or ratios utilizing the data presented in most company financial statements. Complex financial models take into account other kinds of information such as the time value of cash inflows, risk, and the relationship to stockmarket performance. A good painter has an understanding of these techniques and uses them in a creative and pragmatic manner.

Chapter 5

Fundamentals: Experience Curves and Product Life Cycles

A painter has to really understand the color wheel concept before he or she can start painting. It is this knowledge which allows a painter to identify the primary colors, which are then combined to create the intermediate colors. In addition, it allows the painter to identify color complements, which, when placed next to each other, either intensify or neutralize themselves. He or she must also have knowledge of analogous colors, which help to create a harmonious painting.

Similarly, before we can get into what many consider the fun part of strategic planning, strategy formulation, we really need to look at two concepts that can provide us with a basic foundation for understanding how and why we can utilize our strategic options palette. These two concepts are the experience curve and the product life cycle. You have probably heard of them before, but it is important to know their pragmatic uses and how valuable they can be when making strategic choices.

Like all ideas, these concepts have arguments both for and against them and if followed strictly, aren't necessarily applicable in all situations. But, if you understand that business is an art form, not a science, and that in art there are few absolutes, then you can come away with some very useful information.

In order to explain these two concepts, we are going to look at some graphs. Sometimes people get confused when looking at graphs, such as the economic supply and demand curves. They know what they mean, but understanding how they really work and what they are really saying is another thing. Basically, what the supply and demand curve graph illustrates is that at a certain price, supply will equal demand. Or, when people want a certain amount of a product, and you are charging a certain price for that product, you only need to produce a specific amount to have enough for all of the people looking for that product at that price. It is just that simple. So, let's talk about some principles and use some graphs to help us understand them.

The Experience Curve

The Experience curve simply states that the more you do something, the better you get at doing it. Therefore, in manufacturing, for example, the more you make, the better you get at making it and the lower your unit cost. This was first thought to apply only to the labor portion of manufacturing costs. Later, evidence mounted that the phenomenon was broader, including administration, sales, marketing, distribution, etc. Also, the experience effect has been observed in a wide range of products including automobiles, semiconductors, petrochemicals, long distance telephone calls, synthetic fibers, airline transportation, the cost of administering life insurance and crushed lime-stone, just to mention a few. It must be noted that this list includes, but is not limited to, high technology products, services, manufacturing industries, consumer goods, industrial products, new products, mature products, process to assembly oriented products, and any other kinds of goods or services. Obviously, there is a wide range of applicability. The concept of the experience curve was first developed in the aircraft industry during World War II. Studies of military aircraft production costs showed that for each doubling of cumulative total output of an aircraft model, the deflated unit costs were reduced by 20% of the unit cost before doubling.

An experience curve is plotted with the cumulative quantity produced on the horizontal axis and the unit cost on the vertical axis (Figure 5.1).

The experience curve is downward sloping, which means that as cumulative quantity increases, unit cost decreases. This is due to (1) economies of scale, where your fixed costs per unit are spread out as

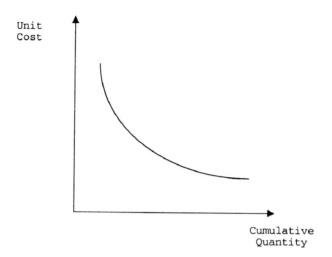

Figure 5.1

the quantity increases and (2) increased efficiency. There is a variety of sources for this downward slope, which are listed below.

Labor Efficiency

As workers repeat a particular production task, they become more dexterous and learn improvements and short cuts which increases their collective efficiency. The greater the number of worker based operations the greater the amount of learning, which can accrue with experience.

Work Specialization and Methods Improvements

Specialization increases worker proficiency at a given task.

Getting Better Performance from Production Equipment

When first designed, a piece of production equipment may have a conservatively rated output. Experience may reveal innovative ways of increasing its output.

Changes in the Resource Mix

As experience accumulates, a producer can often incorporate different or less expensive resources in the operation.

Product Standardization

Standardization allows the replication of tasks, which in turn facilitates worker learning. Production of the Ford Model-T, for example, followed a strategy of deliberate standardization; as a result, from 1909 to 1923 its price was repeatedly reduced following an 85% experience curve.

Product Redesign

As experience is gained with a product, both the manufacturer and customers gain a clearer understanding of its performance requirements. This understanding allows the product to be redesigned to conserve material, allows greater efficiency in manufacturing, and allows for substitution of less costly materials and resources while at the same time improving performance on relevant dimensions.

The above list of sources dramatizes the observation that cost reductions due to experience don't occur by natural inclination; they are the result of substantial, concerted effort to lower costs.

When looking at the illustration of the curve, you can see that it is not a straight line. Instead, it is a downward curving line with a steep decline in the beginning at low cumulative quantity, and it then flattens out as cumulative quantity increases.   Theoretically, the curve never flattens out completely, but in a pragmatic sense, eventually unit cost change becomes negligible.

The experience curve has fluctuations in the line. For example, if a company has made a lot of money, but has many bad managers, their unit cost is not necessarily lower. So, when considering the experience curve here, we are assuming that everything is equal. We are making the same product and using the same process. When we compete, we make the assumption that our competition is as good as we are and can do everything as well as we can, if not better. We can not dominate the competition. We have to outthink them strategically. So in general, the more one produces, the lower the unit costs. The question is what does this all mean to us and how can this idea be pragmatically used. In order to answer these questions, we need to make sure we understand the concept of market share.

Market share is a function of how much you produce. Some people may challenge that statement, saying this is not true since you do not necessarily sell all that you produce; some goes into inventory. My answer is that if you don't eventually sell it, you don't have to worry about the experience curve, since in the real world, if you don't sell it you will not be in business very long. So, we can say that what you produce compared to the sum total of what everyone else produces is your market share. For example, if you produce 25 products and the sum total of all you and your competitors produce is 100, then your market share is 25%.

The next point that is often made is that market share is usually calculated on an annual basis, but cumulative quantity is the total sum of all you have produced. This is a valid point, but for what we are going to use experience curve for, the approximation of cumulative quantity to market share is close enough.

So, based upon this close relationship, we can say that someone at the bottom of the experience curve generally would have a greater market share than someone at the top of the curve, since the person at the bottom of the curve has more cumulative quantity.

Relative Market Share

Except for the market leader, it must be emphasized that market share strategically means very little. As a strategic manager, or as a company C.E.O. that is looking to assure the long-term viability of the company through the process we are discussing, market share means practically nothing. If our market share increases from 10% to 12% it does not necessarily mean that we are earning more money. You could have decreased your unit selling price, which drove up demand. If you have a 10% market share and the nearest competitor has 1% then you are strong strategically. But if you have 10% and your nearest competitor has 20% then you are not very strong. So market share in itself is not a valuable piece of information.

What is a valuable piece of information is relative market share (RMS), which is our market share compared to the market leader.

$$\text{Relative Market Share} = \frac{\text{Our Market Share}}{\text{Leader's Market Share}}$$

The highest value of RMS is 1. If we are the market leader, we have an RMS of 1 (us divided by us) and we are lowest on the curve. If our RMS is a very low number, or we are at the top of the curve and the market leader is at the bottom of the curve, then there is a tremendous cost differential between the market leader and us. If the market leader has an

RMS of 1 and we have an RMS of 0.01, then the market leader has a cost advantage over us. Let's look at an example.

Our market share	=	2%
Leader's market share	=	10%
Our RMS	=	2/10 = 0.2

Industry Types

We can identify three types of industries along the experience curve – mature, transitional, and emerging (See Figure 5.2). If everyone is at the bottom of the curve then it is a very mature industry. They have different market shares, but the companies have all been in the industry for a long time. Note that there is very little cost differential between the companies because they are all toward the bottom of the flattened curve. It is important to recognize this since it indicates that, because our costs are similar, no one in this industry should compete on price. The reason for this is that since all of the competitors have basically the same costs, if one company drops prices everyone else will follow suit. A good example of this was the airline price war, where many companies got caught up in competitive pricing and wound up out of business.

The second type of industry is when everyone is at the top of the curve, indicating that this is an emerging industry. The top of the curve is very steep, illustrating a significant cost differential between the companies. Therefore, the leader has the low-cost producer advantage. This is one of the main reasons it is good to be first in an emerging industry. It is in this situation, and only in this situation, where a low price strategy can be affective. This option of low pricing should only be done by the market leader. For example, my company is the first one in an emerging industry and is therefore the market leader in the business. My cost per unit is $1, and I chose to sell each unit for $5. This would give me a profit of $4 per unit. If another company enters the market and tries to gain market share by incorporating a low price strategy, selling the same product for $3 per unit, they could get into serious trouble. Because they are new to the industry, their costs must be more than mine. Let's say they try to sell at $2 per unit. Apparently they are willing to live with a reduced profit of $1 per unit. However, when my company sees that they are gaining market share, all we have to do is drop our prices to $1.50 per

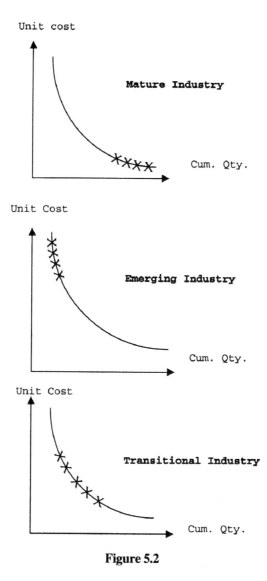

Figure 5.2

unit. We would still be making $.50 per unit. Your company is now in big trouble, because you have just gone from the low-price company to the high-price company, and if you lower your price you will go out of business. You just lost. Only if you have a lot more resources than my company can you try this type of strategy. This is where the term "buying market share" comes from.

Another use for the experience curve in emerging industries is in initial pricing strategies. For example, if your company is the first to enter a market with a new product and your research has developed an acceptable market price that is less than the cost to produce, you can look to the experience curve for help. The curve says that in emerging industries, costs drop rather quickly. Therefore, what you could do is compute how many items you must produce before the product becomes profitable. If you have the reserved resources and if the market is big enough so that you can eventually make a lot of profit, you could decide to enter.

The third type of industry we can identify along the experience curve is the transitional industry. This is an industry where there are both new and experienced competitors. The firms are scattered throughout the curve. The best approach to a low-price strategy is a function of where exactly on the curve these industries are positioned. Generally speaking, once again, a company has to be very careful about selecting a low-price strategy. In this situation, the only company that should even consider this type of strategy should be the market leader.

In situations like those just discussed, if you are in a mature industry, whether or not you're the market leader, what do you do? Well, in that case there is a particular philosophy or rule that you can apply. The rule says, "When you are in a game and you cannot win, change the rules of the game." That does not mean to cheat, it means shift the paradigm. Try going back to the assumption that all companies in the industry have similar skills, products, and processes. The rules can be changed by simply changing the product or the process.

There are other strategic possibilities generated through the understanding and use of the experience curve. Samples of experience curve pricing can be found as early as the Model Ford. Henry Ford experimented with several models until 1908 when he settled on the design for the Model T. Confident that the Model T would open up a large market in a world where the automobile was still a high-priced luxury, he made a commitment to a highly standardized design and geared up for volume production. The sharp price cuts on the Model T in 1908 opened up the era of mass automobile transportation. The considerable growth in volume led to substantial cost reductions and further price cuts. By the early 1920s the real price (net of inflation) had dropped by more than two-thirds, and Ford was the undisputed industry leader with 50% market share.

Not surprisingly, experience curve pricing has been quite common in industries in which the Japanese have achieved export competitiveness. In these cases the relatively sudden entry into foreign markets, often the U.S. market, at price levels well below current industry levels has provoked an emotional reaction. The charge is usually "dumping," that is, selling below full costs in the export market while "taxing" consumers in the protected home market, who pay far more than full cost. The use of experience curve pricing in the export market is a logical extension of the competitive struggle between Japanese firms and non-Japanese firms. Overall volume from all markets, that is, world market shares, determines overall competitive cost differentials and profit potential.

It is also important to remember that successful Japanese penetration has seldom been based entirely on price. The successful Japanese product inevitably provides a user advantage in quality (television sets), or in performance or economy in use (automobiles), or the inclusion of desirable features without price premiums (machine tools). Price and performance characteristics must be viewed as a whole and, for the Japanese too, pricing is only one element in an integrated strategy. However, the Japanese have been known as "market share buyers."

Strategic Implications

Several logical strategic observations can be made about the experience curve. First, the market leader in an industry with the largest market share will have generally produced the largest number of units and should have the lowest cost when all firms are on the same experience curve. Second, if a competitor develops an advantageous process technology or can successfully differentiate its product, it can change the outcome the existing experience curve. Finally, a firm with greater experience can use an aggressive price policy as a competitive weapon to gain even greater market share.

In industries where a significant portion of total cost can be reduced due to the experience curve, important cost advantages can usually be achieved by pursuing a strategy geared to accumulating experience faster than competitors.

The advantage of being the leader is obvious. Leadership is usually best seized at the start when experience doubles quickly (i.e. experience can increase tenfold as you move from the 20th to the 2,000th unit, but only doubles as you move from the 2,000th to the 4,000th unit). Then a firm can build an unassailable cost advantage and at the same time gain price leadership. The best course of action for a product depends on a number of factors, one of the most important being the market growth rate. In fast-growing markets, experience can be gained by taking a disproportionately smallshare of new sales, thereby avoiding taking sales away from competitors (which would be vigorously resisted). Therefore, with high rates of growth, aggressive action may be called for. But, share-gaining tactics are usually costly in the short run, due to reduced margins from lower prices, added advertising to the marketing expense, new product development costs, and the like. This means that if it lacks the resources (product, financial, and other) for leadership, and in particular, if it is opposed to by a very aggressive competitor, a firm may find it wise to abandon the market entirely or focus on a segment it can dominate. On the other hand, in no growth or slowly growing markets it is hard to take market share from competitors, and the time it takes to acquire superior experience is usually too long and the cost too great to favor aggressive pricing strategies.

Another connection between market share and the cost-experience curve is through the interdependent activity of related SBUs. Experience is said to accumulate at the activity level rather than the product level. Therefore, where related SBUs have common activity bases, accumulated experience is compounded, and market share and cost can have a weak relationship.

A portfolio that contains related business units incorporates a natural synergy that provides cost advantages. If products can be designed with economic production methods in mind, cost, compared to competitors, may be advantageous. This concentration on production design becomes even more important as volume increases. It may involve better utilization of materials, or substitution of more economical materials that may make possible lower-cost production methods. Production design may standardize materials and parts so that a wider variety of sizes and types of the product use some of the same parts, allowing higher volume and experience curve effects for those parts and an economy of scale in their manufacture. A company can gain significant operating advantages by integrating manufacturing activities from several business units that use the same or similar processes. Indeed, integration of activities should be a good method for acquisitions, because the "fit" makes good sense and produces a combined unit with cost advantages.

Pros and Cons of the Experience Curve

One of the main functions of the experience curve is that it can and often is used to measure a company's competitive position. This is done through the value of a company's relative market share. The basic idea is that the closer you are to the market leader, the more competitive you are since your costs are among the lowest. The problem with this approach is that in mature industries all of the competitors are at the bottom of the curve, and at this point there is little cost difference between them. So, even if your relative market share is very high, you do not have a significant competitive position. The same is true if you have a low relative market share value. You are not in that weak of a position. However, as long as you understand that this problem exists, utilization of the experience curve can still be affective.

The next two biggest problems with the experience curve concept are the assumptions and the relationship between cumulative quantity and market share. With regards to the assumptions, there are some industries where the product is made in the same manner and is exactly the same no matter who is producing it. Some examples can be found when the customer is either a government agency or an industrial buyer. In these cases, the product must often meets exact production and performance specifications. In addition, there are many food products, including food crops, which are basically the same. In any case, one should start with the assumption that the playing field is level.

With regards to the relationship between cumulative quantity and market share, the company that has produced the most over the years is often the market leader. But, if this is not true, the value for relative market share, which is what we are primarily concerned with, will not be far enough off to make a significant difference when we use it to help paint our strategies.

The key advantage of understanding the experience curve is knowing the futility of trying to compete on price. It is another step toward knowing the strategic palette and therefore understanding all of the other possible ways to compete.

The Product Life Cycle

Like people, products go through changes during their lifetimes. People are born, products are introduced. People grow and multiply, products grow and multiply. People mature, products mature. People grow old and decline, products grow old and decline. People cease to exist, products cease to exist. As a person goes through these different stages, they encounter different circumstances and relate differently to their surrounding environment. What works for a child and allows them to excel, does not necessarily work for them when they become an adult. The same is true of products.

Thus, in order to be successful and meet its full potential, it is critical to identify and understand the stages that products go through as time passes. Any failure to understand these changes and to adjust the company's strategy may result in premature death of a product.

Description

The Product Life Cycle (PLC) identifies four discrete stages of a product: introduction, growth, maturity, and decline. The value on the horizontal axis is "time" and the value on the vertical axis is "revenues." Figure 5.3 illustrates this relationship between revenues, time, and life stages. Some people use "profits" as the variable on the vertical axis, but this is the wrong approach. When developing strategy I do not often discuss profits since profits have very little to do with strategy formulation. Profits are a result of a strategy and not the determinant of a strategy. Profits are dependent upon too many variables to be of much use in strategy development.

The product life cycle curve itself illustrates the relationship between revenues over time. What is that relationship called? If you understand that revenues are the same as sales, you see that the curve represents the change of either revenues or sales over time of a particular product. Remember, the product life cycle is for the entire industry's change of sales over time, which is called the market growth rate.

If you understand that the curve is the change of revenues over time, and that this is the same as the market growth rate, then you should understand that a product's position on the curve is simply determined by knowing its market growth rate. If the market growth rate is high, let's say 10%, then the product is in the growth stage on the product life cycle. If the market growth rate is low, let's say 2%, then the product is in the maturity stage on the product life cycle. If the market growth rate is a fairly high negative number, -9% let's say, then the product is in the decline stage of the product life cycle. People ask, "if the market growth rate is showing a small decline, how do I know if it is in introduction or decline?" My response is that if you do not know if your product is in introduction or decline then you'd better get out of the business.

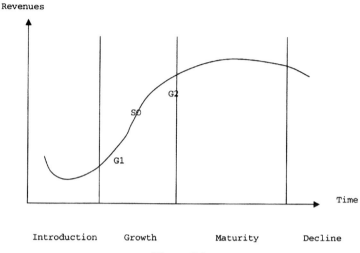

Figure 5.3

Although the product life cycle curve looks smooth, it really is not. Actually, revenues are oscillating over time, being forced up and down because of external factors. For example, if there is bad weather in Brazil, fewer beans will be available for coffee production. Industry sales will temporally decline. When the weather improves, the crop will flourish, coffee beans will be abundant, and revenues will increase. What the product represents is the *average* change in revenues over time. So, do not be confused when the market growth rate is 15% one year, and then – 2% the next year. You really need to know the average market growth rate to determine where the product lies on the life cycle curve.

Also, when looking at the product life cycle graph, you see very thin vertical lines where products go from one stage to another. However, these lines are really not that thin. These are actually really fuzzy lines, meaning that there is no exact moment in time when a product transitions to another stage. Although the different stages look equally divided by the vertical separators, the time periods that they represent are not necessarily equal. Introduction can be very long, growth can be very short, maturity can be very long, and decline can be very short. It all depends on the product. Today, typically, product life cycles are getting shorter and shorter. Companies now have to make sure that there is enough time in maturity to get back their investment plus an expectable profit. Generally, high-tech type products such as computers and electronics have short life cycles and commodities such as iron and wheat have longer life cycles.

Each stage of the product life cycle is explained below in more detail.

Introduction Stage

The first stage of the PLC is introduction. It is at this stage that products first come into the market. Notice the downward slop of the product life cycle curve. This indicates that there is often a negative revenue stream when introducing a new product.

The number of competitors during introduction is at a minimum, as businesses are often reluctant to take the risk, and face the cost of being innovators.

Growth Stage

The growth stage can be characterized by the product's market acceptance and most importantly, the furious level of competition. When companies start seeing a product's high growth, there is often a mad rush to enter the fray. Therefore, because of the high level of competition, it is important to look very closely at what is occurring. A company's survival depends upon how well it is prepared for this intense stage of a product's life cycle.

Accordingly, I have divided the growth stage into two separate stages (Figure 5.3). G1 is the designation for growth one. Note that the curve is sloping upward here and is becoming almost vertical. This is because at this time revenues are increasing at an increasing rate. You can imagine the number of competitors who will enter the industry when they see a market that is growing exponentially. G2 is the designation for growth two. Here the curve is sloping upward, but it is starting to flatten out. Although revenues are still increasing in G1, they are now increasing at a decreasing rate. The mid-point, between GI and GII, is the point of inflection. It is here where the curve changes from increasing at an increasing rate to increasing at a decreasing rate. Growth is always occurring through out this stage, it is just the rate of increase that is changing.

A unique occurrence during the growth stage is an event called industry shakeout. Industry shakeout often takes place sometime between

G1 and G2. This is designated by the "SO" mark on the curve. What is occurring is a result of the exponential high growth of G1. Because of this growth, usually there are a large number of companies who decide to jump into the market, which results in over-capacity. The result is that only the well prepared survive. The unprepared are "shaken out" of the business. You can see this occurring all the time in new industries when they go into high growth. Apple was the first to enter the personal computer business. As soon as Apple was doing well and it appeared that the personal computer was here to stay, IBM jumped in. As growth soared, many other companies tried to get a piece of the action. Today, most of them are no longer around. They were the ones not prepared for growth.

Maturity Stage

The maturity stage is defined as the period when the industry goes from low growth to no growth and begins to regress. It is the time of highest revenues where companies reap the rewards for surviving the wars of growth. Very small changes in market share are accompanied by high changes in revenues. Companies often focus on extending this stage for as long as possible.

The number of competitors is usually stable, with very few firms entering or leaving the industry. Calculators and watches are examples of mature businesses. At the peak, there were hundreds of competitors. Now only a handful of strong competitors remain. The stable condition is caused by a number of entry barriers, consisting of strong brand loyalty, an established mass distribution network, and the full product line necessary in the highly segmented and highly competitive markets.

A major strategic concern for companies in this stage is determining how long maturity will last. For some industries such as basic commodities, this stage can go on almost indefinitely. For other products, the time of maturity can be very short. This is especially true in today's high-tech, fast paced world. In this case, companies have to develop strategies that will allow them to either extend maturity, or prepare the company for decline.

The automobile has been in the maturity stage for many decades. Whether it may enter the decline stage or not depends on whether a new, better, faster, and more economical mode of transportation is feasible. If objects and people could be beamed from place to place, automobiles and airplanes would have seen their better day.

Decline Stage

The decline stage is exemplified by a constant increase in the rate of declining revenues. It is a time of great concern since it could signal the end of the company. Because of this, there are many books with tons of strategies showing you the way to save your company. I have always been a little pessimistic about generic strategies. It seems to me that every situation is different. When you are sick and are told to take an aspirin and go to bed, everything won't necessarily be fine in the morning. Before you can prescribe the antidote, you need to diagnose the illness. The same is true in business. Before you can select the right strategy, you have to know the reason why the industry is in decline.

After much research and careful observation, I have concluded that there are three reasons for decline. The first is technological obsolescence, the second is the substitution effect, and the third is that the total demand has been met.

In the first case, technological obsolescence, the most appropriate approach would be product innovation. If there is a better product out there that is putting you out of business, it's time to change. As obvious as this may seem, there are still companies out there who will not accept the message. Before transistors there were vacuum tubes. When transistors came out, the vacuum tube people decided that the way to respond was to make vacuum tubes more efficiently. They eventually reached the conclusion that transistors were here to stay and that this strategy was not going to work.

In the second case, the substitution effect, the most appropriate approach would be process innovation. What is occurring at this time is that other companies have discovered another product that is currently being used for something else can be used to meet the needs currently being met by your product. This is probably due to cost and capabilities. What is needed is a new process to manufacture your product in a less expensive manner.

The third case, filled demand, can be responded to by numerous approaches. For example, you can get out of the business by either liquidation or selling the company. Another approach would be just the opposite, where you could buy all the competition, probably at discounted prices, and be one of the few remaining producers This is a time when you will have to be a very creative painter.

Strategic Implications

As with the experience curve, if you don't like the game or stage of the product life cycle that you are in, you can change the rules. In this case you can actually change the position of a product on the product life cycle, through marketing. One approach is to change your target segment. Your product may be in maturity in the United States, but no one else has heard of it. If you change your target segment from just the US to the world, you could move the product back to growth.

Another approach would be to make people feel that your product is something other than what they thought it was. The classic example of this is baking soda. Historically, baking soda was just used for cooking. Now it is considered a great deodorant and is used in such things as toothpaste. It is still the same product, but people perceive it as something else.

The product life cycle is a very important tool in the painting of your picture. It shows you which of the colors on your palette should be considered first. In other words, different strategies are appropriate as products pass through their life cycles. Marketing would be different for a product in G1 versus a product in maturity. Figure 5.4 illustrates the primary considerations for each of the areas on your palette as your product move through the different life cycle stages. Please do not think that these are exclusive considerations. For example, the primary marketing consideration for a product in introduction should be product development. When you are introducing a new product it is important to make sure that it is what your new customers want and need. As the product goes through Growth, the marketing effort should now be focused on promotion. This is the highest level of competition, and you must get people to recognize the value of your product. Next, when the product is in maturity, the focus should be on distribution, since you are now selling to a mass audience. Finally, in decline, as it has been stated, the appropriate strategy is a function of the cause of decline. When faced with the substitution effect, one strategy would be to promote the value of your product which is being substituted. However, as stated, these are not mutually exclusive approaches. You must consider all of the elements pertaining to marketing that are on your palette. Obviously price is something to look at all the time. Promotion has an impact in all stages. But, those in Figure 5.4 are the first that you should look at.

	Introduction	Growth	Maturity	Decline
Marketing	product	promotion	distribution	product
Production	facilities/location	cap./processes	mat'ls hand./sched	cap./processes
Research & Development	product	process	prod/proc	processes
Financial	cash flow	cash flow	cash handling	cash handling
Human Resource Management	staffing	staffing	mot./leadership	staffing
Management Information Systems	hard/software	info. dist.	info. dist.	hard/software
Organization Design	structure	structure	communication	structure

Figure 5.4

Pros and Cons of the PLC

The pros of the product life cycle are obvious. It is a tool which provides you with an understanding of expected revenues and applicable strategic approaches.

However, there are some arguments against it. For one, some argue that all products do not go through all the stages. They say for example, that wheat has and never will go into decline just like all other products. Those taking this position are confused by the time variable on the horizontal axis. Wheat, will eventually go into decline. Tomorrow, some scientist might invent a synthetic substitute and wheat, and all the problems that are associated with growing it, will be gone. I can just hear some Roman centurian arguing that chariots will be around forever. Time on the life cycle can be very long as with wheat, or very short as with many of today's high tech products. In addition, some argue that a product can be introduced, go into growth and then right into decline, with no maturity. They do not understand that the time segments of the product life cycle are not equal. A particular stage may be very, very short, but it is there.

Knowing and, more importantly, understanding the PCL can be very advantageous. The volume of information that the PCL provides cannot be ignored. Expected future revenues, the level of competition, and the appropriate "colors," or strategic choices from your palette are only some of the kinds of information that can be gleamed from a pragmatic understanding of the PCL.

Summary

Like the color wheel concept that the painter should understand, strategic planners should understand the experience curve and product life cycle concepts.

The Experience Curve displays a company's competitive advantage due to cost. On the vertical axis unit cost is measured, and on the horizontal axis cumulative quantity is measured. The Experience Curve is downward sloping which illustrates the concept that as cumulative quantity increases, unit cost decreases. In other words, the more you make the lower your costs. The major reasons for the downward slope is the economies of scale and efficiency. We can relate cumulative quantity to market share, which strategically means very little. What is important is relative market share, which is our market share compared to that of the market leader. The value of the relative market share ranges from 0 to 1. If a company is the market leader, their relative market share is 1.

There are three categories of industries that we can identify along the experience curve. A mature industry is one where all the competitors are at the bottom of the curve. They have very little cost differentials between them and they have a lot of experience in the particular industry. These industries should not compete on price, not even the market leader.

The second category of industry is one where all of the competitors are at the top of the curve. This illustrates an emerging industry. The top of the curve is very steep, which indicates a significant cost differential. Here there is an advantage available to the first company in the industry, the market leader, who has a tremendous competitive advantage.

The third category is the transitional industry where everyone is scattered throughout the curve, and nobody has much experience in making the product. In this case there can only be a cost advantage if there is a significant relative market share difference.

The PLC says that all products go through a series of evolutionary stages: introduction, growth, maturity, and decline. The PLC measures revenues on the vertical axis and time on the horizontal axis. Revenues are very low during introduction, increase during growth, begin to level off during maturity, and decline during the declining stage.

The PLC relates to market growth rate, which is the difference in revenues over time. The growth stage is split into two stages, growth one (G1) and growth two (G2). In G1, revenues are increasing at an increasing rate and in G2, revenues are increasing at a decreasing rate. Somewhere in between these two stages products go through a shake out. G1 is the stage of highest competition, and those who survive this go through G2.

All products eventually will go into decline. There are three reasons why products do so. The first is technological obsolescence. Here, a better product has been made, and a strategy you should first consider is product innovation. The second reason for decline is the substitution effect where another product has been substituted for your product. The first consideration here should be process innovation. The third reason for decline is that there is no more demand for that particular product. There are several possibilities for this situation.

Each functional area on our palette plays a different part during each stage of the PLC. This is due to the nature of the competition and revenue stream. All elements should be considered, but certain ones should be reviewed as the most likely to have impact.

Finally, although there is some disagreement surrounding the experience curve and product life cycle, there is still much to be gained through their informed and pragmatic application.

Chapter 6

Painting Techniques:
Portfolio Modeling

So far, we've laid out our palette, set the parameters for our painting, defined specifically what we wanted to accomplish, reviewed our own capabilities, looked at what others have done, and sketched in an idea of what we might paint. Now it is time to develop some specific techniques to plot out the great strategy that can lead your company to success and long-term viability.

Each particular style in art has special techniques that the artist uses to achieve desired results, much like the techniques that the strategic planner can use to mix the strategic palette colors. This technique is portfolio modeling and through its proper use, you too can become a better "painter."

In Chapter 4, we sketched in our painting with financial models. From the first chapter we remember that what we were doing was allocating the company's resources. Portfolio models allow you to continue that process and also to go a little further, pointing out which colors will provide you with the ability to fill in the rest of the painting. They can help the strategic planner make the correct choices from the right side (competitive strategies) of the palette.

There are many variations of portfolio models. Like financial models, consulting firms dream them up so they can have a distinctive approach when marketing their services. As we have discussed, all models have pros and cons. The consulting firms are also aware of this. So what they do is look at the negatives of a model and then build one of their own, which will compensate for the negatives of the model used by their competition. Even though there are many variations, most portfolio models are similar in that they utilize two variables. One is a measure of market performance, and a second, is a measure of company performance. In addition, unlike financial models, they all consider the synergies between the products and the strategic business units (SBUs).

Two of the most often discussed are the Boston Consulting Group four cell model and the McKinsey/GE nine-cell model. Although there are others, we will discuss these two in this chapter.

Before I start the discussion about the Boston Consulting Group matrix and the McKinsey nine-cell matrix, I have to admit that many practitioners and faculty have asked me why I focus on these two matrixes. They are, in fact, old and some question their relevance. I respond with a two-part answer. First, although most people in business had heard of these matrixes, they often never really understood them. They just memorized the description without developing an in-depth understanding of how they work and how they should be interpreted. Hopefully, after our discussion, you will come to really know what they are telling you, while taking into account their good points and bad points. By knowing both, you will come to appreciate their value as I have. Second, these two matrixes form the foundation of portfolio models. So, if you get to know and understand them, they can serve as a guide to make your own model that would work even better for your organization. Let's begin by looking at the more basic of the two models, Boston Consulting Group Matrix.

The Boston Consulting Group Matrix

The Boston Consulting Group designed the Boston Consulting Group Matrix (BCG) for large corporations to have a graphical representation of their firm's SBUs with regard to competitiveness versus market desirability, and SBU importance.

The construction of the BCG Matrix grid that we will use is fairly simple and will use terminology that you will recognize from the product life cycle and the experience curve.

In the previous chapter we talked about the experience curve. We associated the experience curve with relative market share, noting that the larger the value, up to 1 for the market leader, the more cost competitive we are. The BCG matrix uses this concept to measure competitiveness, which is on the horizontal axis, with relative market share. Again, the higher our relative market share, the more competitive we are.

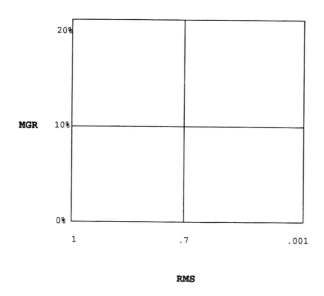

RMS

Boston Consulting Group Four-Cell Matrix
Figure 6.1

Also, in the previous chapter, we talked about the product life cycle. We came to understand that the slope of the life cycle curve illustrated the change of revenues over time, which we then related to the market growth rate. The BCG also uses market growth rate. The premise being that if an industry is in growth it is a good industry to be in, and if it is in decline it is not so good to be in. Note that I did not say that it is "bad" to be in, just "not so good."

These two variables are plotted against each other in a four-cell matrix (Figure 6.1). You can see that the vertical axis showing market growth rate is split into two, making up two upper boxes and two lower boxes. The upper two boxes are those where market growth is greater than 10%. The lower two boxes are those where market growth is less than 10%. The premise being that markets with growth rates greater than 10% are markets with strong growth and therefore are good ones to be in, while markets with growth rates less than 10% are markets that do not exhibit significant growth and are therefore not desirable. You can also see that the top boundary is 20% and that the bottom boundary is 0%. The question arises as to what to do if you are in an industry that has a higher growth rate than 20%, or is in decline, with a negative growth rate. The answer is to simply change these values. It really makes· no difference what either of these high-low end point values are. However, do not change the dividing value of 10%. It is important to realize that 10% is the dividing line between high and low growth, or good markets and not so good markets. When you change the end points you are still illustrating the concept that above 10% is good and below 10% is not so good. But, if you change the mid-point value of 10%, you then change the concept. If you, let's say for example, change the mid-point value to 20% in order to have a nice symmetrical matrix, you would be saying that markets with an 18% growth rate are not so good to be in, and this would be contrary to the premise of the matrix.

Now let's look at the horizontal axis, which is using relative market share (RMS) to measure competitiveness. In the previous chapter we said that relative market share is computed by dividing our market share by the market leader's market share. If we are the market leaders, then the computation would be us divided by ourselves, and that value would be 1. Therefore, the most competitive position with regards to cost and pricing ability would be to the left of the matrix.

Sometimes you do see this matrix with the left extreme value greater than one. What is occurring here is that instead of comparing your SBU to the market leader, you are comparing it to the nearest competitor. This is sometimes done when most of the competing companies are all far away from the market leader and you are trying to see how cost competitive you are compared to the industry majority.

On the other end, note that the value is .001. This is some value greater than zero, because technically, if the extreme value were zero, then you would have no market share at all, and the matrix would not be applicable.

The most interesting point is the dividing point that separates the competitive SBUs and the ones that are not so competitive. Sometimes you will see this value as .5. The only reason for this as far as I can tell is to establish symmetry, but symmetry is not important. The idea being illustrated is that if an SBU falls into any of the left two boxes, they are very competitive. If they fall into the right two boxes, they are not so competitive. Therefore, the value of .7 is used, being a more realistic indication of what is or is not competitive. The value of .7 is more realistic because the experience curve is in fact a curve that flattens out at the bottom. Businesses whose relative market share is close to 1 are often grouped at this flat bottom section. So even though their RMS is a little less than 1, their unit cost is not much less than the market leader. Therefore they are fairly cost competitive.

SBU	Revenue	size
1	$20M	
2	$10M	
3	$5M	

$35M   Total Company Revenues

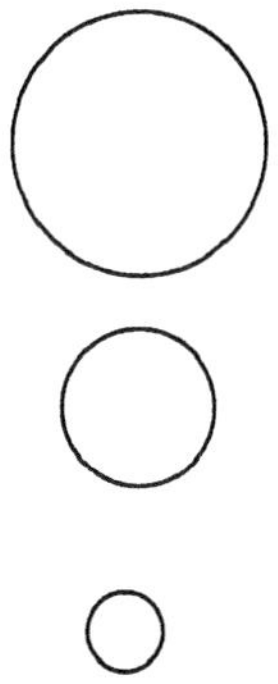

Relative Circle Size Utilizing Total Company Revenues
Figure 6.2

There is one other part to the BCG matrix and that involves how each SBU is represented once it is plotted. Circles are used instead of simply having a dot representing each business unit. These circles vary in size. The size represents the revenue contribution of the individual business unit as compared to the others. The largest circle represents the SBU with the largest revenues. The remaining SBU circles should be represented in direct proportion to the largest circle. Let's take ACME Corporation for an example. ACME has three SBU's (see Figure 6.2). Notice that SBU1, which has the largest revenues for the company, is the largest circle. SBU2, which is contributing half the amount of revenues as SBU1, is represented by a circle half the size of the one representing SBU1. SBU3 contributes half, $5M, of what

SBU2 is contributing, so it is half the size of SBU2's circle.   The importance of this is that by simply looking at the circles you can tell which SBU is the largest revenue contributor, and knowing this would have a great impact upon your strategy selection. For example, you would tend to have more conservative strategies for large contributors, and more radical strategies would be acceptable for SBU's that are not significant contributors.   The final BCG matrix will now look like the one in Figure 6.3.

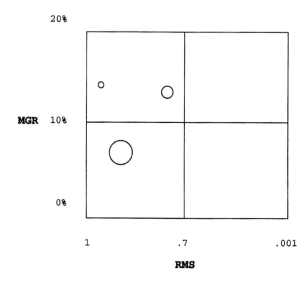

Completed BCG Matrix
Figure 6.3

The BCG in Depth Analysis

Now that this tool is reviewed, the central question is what does it all mean.   How can it help us paint?   Before that question is answered, an explanation is required first about what it does not mean. To facilitate the practitioner's use of the matrix, there was an attempt to simplify it.   This has resulted in a lot of confusion regarding its efficiency.   Each quadrant was given a label that was used as a description of the appropriate strategy that should be used for any SBU falling into a quadrant. The top left quadrant was labeled "stars." The top right quadrant was labeled "question marks." The bottom left quadrant was labeled "cash cows," and the bottom right quadrant was labeled "dogs."

These names were not arbitrarily given. The idea was that an SBU falling into the top left star quadrant was one that was in high market growth and one where the company held a competitive low-cost advantage, thus, the name star. An SBU falling into the top right quadrant was one that was in a high growth market, but one where the company did not hold a competitive low-cost advantage, thus the name question mark. An SBU falling into the bottom left quadrant was one that was in a low growth market and one where the company held a competitive low-cost advantage. Remember that a low growth market is probably one that is in maturity and therefore one where there are high revenues. Also, if according to the experience curve, you have high relative market share, then your costs are relatively low. Thus, in the bottom left quadrant you have an SBU that has high revenues and low cost or, in other words, a cash cow. Finally, SBUs residing in the bottom right corner are ones with low growth and ones where you are not cost competitive. These are the dogs. To make it simple, one was told to "milk your cash cows, divest your dogs, support your stars, and look closely at your question marks." If you really understand what the matrix represents you know that this simple approach will not work. Forget the stars and animals. You are too smart to need them.

Rather than just memorizing theories about "stars" and "dogs," when you analyze you company utilizing the BCG matrix what you need to consider is what it really means to have an SBU in a specific quadrant. SBUs falling into the top left quadrant are ones that are in high growth. We said before that high growth means that this SBU is in a highly competitive environment. This intense competition demands large cash investments to support expansion. Sometimes, these businesses generate enough cash to maintain their high share of the market, especially since, according to their RMS, they are cost leaders. Yet often, these businesses can not support their investment needs totally from within, but require infusions of investment funds from the other SBUs.

Any SBU located in the lower left quadrant would be generating significant revenues for that market, and would be the market leader or close to the market leader. Because of experience, they would have lower costs. Typically these businesses bring in much more cash than is necessary for maintaining their market share. They can provide cash for financing new business acquisitions and offer financial support to other SBUs in need of cash for expansion or survival. However, a cause for concern would be their future. Are they going to be around for a while, or are they about to go into a quick decline?

The upper right quadrant represents high growth and low relative market share. SBUs falling into this quadrant are in a highly competitive and thus costly environment. To make matters worse, their RMS is less than .7, which places them further away from the market leader's cost advantages. Therefore, unless a strategy can be developed to increase their competitiveness and unless the company has other SBUs that are generating a lot of cash, these SBUs can be in serious trouble. But growth markets are hard to come by so it is important to see what can be done to support these businesses.

Finally, the lower right quadrant represents slow growth and low relative market share. Of all the quadrants, this is the one that presents the most diverse interpretation. In the traditional simplistic analysis, this was the dog quadrant, which was the one you were supposed to divest. But, low growth would indicate that the SBU is in a mature industry, and recalling the Experience Curve analysis, mature industries are ones where all of the competitors are at the bottom of the Experience Curve. So even though this SBU is exhibiting low RMS, it does not necessarily mean that it is a poor performer. Because the curve is so flat here, cost differential is not a good measure of performance. If it is determined that the market is in a long stable maturity stage, then the traditional inclination to divest is incorrect. Instead, this is an SBU that can provide a significant contribution to your company's possibilities.

All of the above analyses are a reflection of the interaction between the two variables of relative market share and market growth rate. But the real use of the BCG matrix is to analyze the inter-relationships between the SBUs, in other words, their synergism. To do this you not only have to consider the impact of RMS and MGR, but you have to look at the impact of the relative location of all of the business units and their relative financial impact.

For example, is it good or bad to have all of the SBUs located in the upper left quadrant. Initially you might think so, but understanding that because they are all in high growth, they are all in intensely competitive markets. It would probably not be a very good idea to fight life and death struggles with all of your SBUs at the same time. The probability of success would not be very high.

How about if all of your SBUs are in the bottom left quadrant? At first, this would seem good because you would be pulling in a lot of revenues. However, with nothing in a growth market, you chances for increasing revenues are not too good. Again, long term success would not be very high.

It should be obvious that your business units should be spread out over the matrix, with no one quadrant accounting for all of your SBU's. In addition, the size of the circles becomes important since, for example, it would probably not be good to have your largest circle in the top left quadrant, high growth, where you are fighting an intense competitive battle, and have a very small circle in the bottom left. With this scenario, your main SBU in growth would be hard pressed for needed resource. No one wants to be in that position. So, be smart, *understand* the matrix and use it to help you paint.

Pros and Cons

The con, or negative aspect, of the matrix is that it only utilizes one measure to determine your performance and if you are in a good industry. It doesn't take much to argue that these are weak measures and that it takes more than one element to determine the viability of the market and your relative competitiveness. As it has been mentioned many times so far, there is no perfect tool and no perfect solution. For every choice there are pros and cons. The BCG's pros is that it is very simple. By looking at, analyzing, and understanding it, you can quickly get a good idea of how your business units are interacting and what some of the strategic possibilities are.

The Nine-Cell Business Strength/Industry Attractiveness Matrix

In order to compensate for the problems of the BCG matrix, General Electric and the McKinsey and Company consulting firm developed the nine-cell portfolio matrix based on the product-market attractiveness and business strength/competitive position. This is sometimes referred to as the G E/McKinsey matrix or more often, the Nine-Cell Industry Attractiveness/Business Strength Matrix. This matrix is a three by three matrix consisting of nine cells. The variable on the vertical axis is "industry attractiveness," and the variable of the horizontal axis is "business strength (see Figure 6.4). Unlike the BCG matrix, which may use a single measure for evaluating the value of the industry and competitiveness, these variables are a measure with a compilation of several factors. Those factors are then weighted as to their relative importance, and then the SBU is evaluated utilizing those weighted factors.

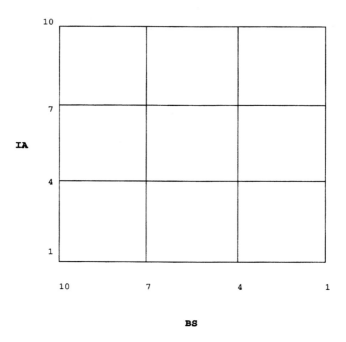

Nine Cell Business Strength/Industry Attractiveness Matrix
Figure 6.4

Rating Business Strength

To rate an SBU's business strength, you first need to develop those criteria necessary for any SBU to successfully compete in its industry. These criteria can be found by looking at other companies, conducting industry research, or by obtaining the opinions of industry experts. These criteria must be very specific and not very broad based.

For example, marketing is too broad, but advertising is a valid measuring tool. All of these factors are elements of the internal environment and are controllable by the company. You should have evaluated them when you were conducting the internal analysis part of your environmental scanning.

Example Domestic Auto SBU

Criteria	Wt.	Rate	Total
Quality control	.3	7	2.1
Automated production systems	.1	8	.8
Distribution network	.3	9	2.7
Advertising campaign	.2	8	1.6
Design engineering	.1	7	.7
Totals	**1.0**		**7.9**

BUSINESS STRENGTH

Descriptors	Wt.	Rate	Total
Transportation	.3	9	2.7
Oligopolistic	.1	9	.9
Mass market	.15	8	1.2
Domestic consumer	.2	8	1.6
Petroleum dependent	.25	4	1.0
Totals	**1.0**		**7.4**

INDUSTRY ATTRACTIVENESS

Example SBU
Figure 6.5

The next step is to list all of the criteria and then to weight them as to their relative importance, remembering that the sum of all the parts need to equal 1. Some promoters of this matrix suggest that a generic list of criteria be developed that is applicable to all industries. Then when you weigh them, you measure those that are not applicable with a zero so that they have no impact on the final calculations. I am not in strong agreement with the generic concept. If you truly wish to be competitive, then you need to develop an understanding of those factors necessary to be competitive. By utilizing good research and good experts, you should be able to come up with a list of those particular criteria necessary to be competitive.

After you have developed the criteria, give them their relative weights and check to make sure that the sum of all the weights equals 1; you are then ready to rate each criteria. You can elect to rate using any scale, but the one used most often seems to be 1 to 10. Your matrix must reflect this same scale. Figure 6.4 illustrates the 1 to 10 scale.

The final step is to multiply the weights times the rates and add all the rates together, giving you a final business strength rating for the SBU. An example of this process is illustrated in Figure 6.5. For our example company, we developed an SBU for the domestic auto industry. Our research and experts in our example industry helped us determine that in order to be competitive you need to have good quality control, automated production systems, distribution network, an advertising campaign, and design engineering. There are more criteria, but for our example SBU we will stop with these five.

We then weighed the criteria as to their relative importance and then rated our SBU for each of the criteria. Our final rating for business strength was 7.9. This is where we would plot this SBU on the horizontal axis illustrating "business strength."

Rating Industry Attractiveness

After we have completed our rating process, we then start a similar procedure to determine how attractive the industry is for the SBU. To do this we first have to develop a set of descriptors, are characteristics to describe the industry. They are no different than describing this book. For example, we could describe the book as being made out of paper, having typewritten words, and providing a message or information. To describe an industry, you need to determine those things that make that industry stand out from the others. Unlike the criteria for business strength which are controllable since they come from the internal environment, the industry descriptors are uncontrollable as they come from the external environment.

In our domestic auto example our descriptors were transportation, oligopoly, mass market, domestic consumer, and petroleum dependent (Figure 6.5). If you were to ask someone what industry you were describing and gave them these five descriptors, they should be able to guess that it is the domestic automobile industry. You could use more descriptors, but, for our example, we will stop at five.

The next step is to weigh each descriptor for its relative importance in describing the industry.

After weighing, we once again rate each descriptor. But, in this step we do something a little bit different. With business strength criteria we simply evaluated our company's performance in each of the criteria; with descriptors we must ask two questions. The first question is how does this descriptor fit with all of our other SBU's. For example, if a descriptor for this SBU were "oligopolistic" and our other SBUs were oligopolistic they would have a pretty good synergistic relationship. If this is the only oligopolistic industry that we are in, then it would not be a very synergistic relationship. We then make the rating. Let's say in our example, that all of our other SBU's are in oligopolistic industries, so we give an initial rating of 10 out of 10. Now we ask a second question; Is it good for us to be alone in an oligopolistic industry? In our example we can assume that we are a large company and generally, for large companies, it is favorable to be in oligopolistic industries. If we were small, we would probably not have enough resources, so oligopolies would not be to good for us. In our case, for this question we give ourselves a rating of 8 out of 10. We are big, but not the biggest. Together, we have two rating of 10 and 8. The average of the two is 9, so that is our rating for this descriptor. We then repeat the process for the rest of the descriptors. After completing the ratings, we once again multiply the weights times the rates and get our totals. The totals are then added which gives us our final rating. In our example, industry attractiveness for the domestic auto industry is 7.4. This is where we would plot this SBU on the vertical axis to illustrate "industry attractiveness" (Figure 6.5).

Now that we have developed both the business strength and the industry attractiveness ratings, we can make the plot on our matrix. This will put this SBU in the top left-hand box of the matrix.

SBU	Industry Revenues	SBU Revenues	Market Share	Size (Potential)
1	$50B	$10B	20%	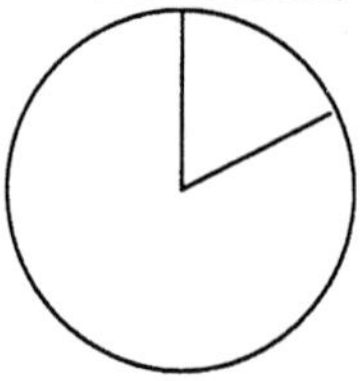
2	$25B	$5B	20%	
3	$15B	$5B	33%	

Market Potential Calculations
Figure 6.6

For the Nine-Cell Business Strength/Industry Attractiveness Matrix, the box in the top left corner is the best to be in since business units in this box are very competitive and in highly attractive industries. The two adjacent boxes, the one to the right and the one below are also good to have SBUs in, but not as good as the top left. Just the opposite is true with the boxes at the bottom right of the matrix. The worst box is the one at the bottom right corner, where an SBU in this box is neither competitive nor in a good industry. The one above it and the one to the left of it are also poor boxes to have SBUs in, but not as bad as the corner box. Any SBUs that reside in any of the three boxes on the diagonal from top right to bottom left are marginal and are neither good nor bad. Unlike the BCG matrix, it is good to have all of your company's SBUs in the top left box. But, before we can make our analysis, there is still one more step to complete.

After all of the company's SBUs are plotted on the matrix, the plot points have to be changed, like the BCG matrix, into circles. However, these circles have a totally different meaning than those in the BCG matrix. Unlike the BCG circles that represent the relative financial importance of each SBU, the circles in this matrix represent the SBU's *potential.* Potential refers to how much opportunity for expansion is there.

Potential is illustrated in the following manner. First, the total revenues for the industry of each SBU are found. Then, the circles are drawn so that their sizes reflect the relative size of the industry as compared to the industries of the other SBUs. Next, the amount of revenue contribution of the SBU is shaded as a pie slice of the circle. This shaded area therefore represents the market share of the SBU. The unshaded area now represents the available market share, or the "potential" (Figure 6.6).

The Nine-Cell BS/IA In-depth Analysis

When developing strategy, it is important to know the potential of an SBU since you probably would not want to recommend a costly high-risk strategy for an SBU with little potential. However, the location of the SBU in the matrix must also be given consideration. SBU's with high potential that are in attractive industries, but are not operating as competitively as they should, should probably get a lot of attention. On the other hand, if an SBU is in an unattractive industry, has little potential, and is one that is not operating competitively, it might be one that could be divested.

When considering which SBU will receive what resources it is also important to consider where *within* an SBU to place those resources. Very often there are a lot of alternatives. One technique is to first review each of the SBU's business strength criteria, determining which of them has the lowest rates. These are obviously areas where you are not performing well. Then look at the weights of these performers. If there is a poor performing criteria, and if it has a high weight, then this probably is an area for creative strategic alternatives. There may be other criteria that also have low weights and low rates, but you should place your resources in areas where you can get, "the most bang for you buck." For example, looking at the SBU in Figure 6.5, you can see that both "quality control" and "design engineering" are rated the lowest with a rate of 7. However, the weight of "quality control" is .3 while the weight of "design engineering" is only .1. If we could only invest in a strategy for one or the other, then it probably would be best to focus on "quality control" since every point that our strategy enables us to raise the rating, our total competitiveness increases by .3. On the other hand, for every point that a strategy for "design engineering" raises our rating, our total competitiveness only increases by .1. Therefore, it appears that the best recommendation would be to adjust the strategy for this SBU by improving quality control. However, before you can make this recommendation you need to consider all of the information that we have developed about the company and this SBU, including the company's financial position, the SBU's financial performance, information from the product life cycle analysis, information from the experience curve analysis, and information from the BCG matrix. You need to consider all of these, and then paint!

The Future Nine-Cell BS/IA Matrix

There is still one more additional step that can be taken which will enable us to get even more information from the nine-cell matrix. The one which we have just completed provided information on the industry attractiveness and our competitiveness today. However, when we implement our strategy, things might have changed. Therefore, we can and should project this matrix into the future to see if the industry attractiveness is going to be less attractive, more attractive, or the same.

Future Industry Attractiveness

Go back to the list of industry attractiveness characteristics and make two additional columns. Label one "future weight" and the other "future total." The scenarios that you developed from your environmental scanning should then be reviewed and you should reconsider the weights of each characteristic. If the industry has changed, then one or some of these should be impacted. This would then require changing its weight and the weight of others since their sum must remain equal to 1.

Referring to our domestic auto SBU example in Figure 6.5, let's say that our future scenario says that the auto industry will change its gasoline engine to one that will use ethanol just as efficiently. In that case the description "petroleum dependent" will not be as important when describing the industry. Therefore, the weight should change. Accordingly, we changed the weight from .25 to .05. But, we can't stop there. Our total weight is now only .8, so we need to adjust the other weights. What we can do is spread the .2 out between the other four descriptions, changing their weights proportionally. So, "transportation" would go from a weight of .3 to .35, "oligopolistic" would go from a .1 to a .15, "mass market" would go from a .15 to a .2, and "domestic consumer" would go from a .2 to a .25. When adding these new weights together, we still get a total of 1. However, our new total industry attractiveness value would now change from a 7.4 to an 8.3. So, if the industry would be less petroleum dependent, it would be a more attractive one.

Future Business Strength

The business strength/competitiveness criteria list will also have two additional columns, but these columns will be labeled "future rate" and "future total." Notice that the rate is changing here, since it was the weight that changed when projecting industry attractiveness. The reason for this is that a rate representing our performance will change for a particular criterion if we change the strategy for that criterion.

Once again, referring to our Domestic Auto SBU example in Figure 6.5, let's say that we decided to focus on a strategy of quality control. Therefore, since we would be getting better at quality control, our SBU's rating would change. The amount of change would be a function of our commitment to that strategy. If our commitment were strong, we could change our rating from its current 7 to a 9. This would result in an increase in total business strength from 7.9 to 8.5.

As with the present nine-cell BS/IA matrix, the future matrix's SBUs are represented by circles with shaded areas. However, these circles could now be very different. To compute the new relative sizes of the circles simply multiply the current industry revenues by the projected market growth rates. These growth rates will probably be different, so the circles' relative sizes will change accordingly. Also, the shaded areas will change; this change is a function of our projected gain in market share. By plotting our new SBU positions on the matrix and employing our new circles and shaded areas, we have created a picture of what our company will look like in the future after we have implemented our new strategies.

Note that for the future nine-cell matrix, only the industry attractiveness weights have been changed. This is the most probable scenario since those attributes, which make the industry attractive or not attractive for you today, are probably the same as they will be in the future. However, this is not always true. For example, let's say that you had an SBU that was in an industry that was described as "industrial consumers" and you rated this high because all of the rest of SBUs were ones that were business to business suppliers. Then, you decided to change your approach and start selling to the mass consumer market. This description would no longer be such a good fit, and your future rating would go down. For this to work, you should have changed your mission statement where you specified who your customers were. That would be the first sign that you need to change both the weights and the rates when projecting industry attractiveness. But, normally this scenario does not occur too often.

A similar situation can occur with business strengths. The original assumption was that your strategy would affect your ratings, but the weights would stay the same, understanding that what it took to be competitive today is what it would take to be competitive tomorrow. This also, may not necessarily be true. An example would be if you were in an industry where the products were all handmade. New technology is discovered which will allow you to automate the production process. Prior to this technological advance, any company that wanted to be competitive need skilled workers, so that was one of the criteria used in the business strength chart. When the industry moves to mass production, this criterion's weight has to change. Perhaps it becomes totally irrelevant, in which case, the weight would go to zero.

Don't think that you cannot add new criteria, or for that matter, new descriptors - you can. The assumption would be that they were there all the time, but were weighted at zero. Also, you could add new SBUs or divest an SBU. The future matrix would now either include the new one or not contain the divested one.

The Future Nine-Cell BS/IA In-Depth Analysis

The future nine-cell matrix provides you with two additional bits of very important information. By changing the industry attractiveness criteria, you will see if the industry will be more or less attractive in the future. By changing the business strength criteria, you will see the impact of your strategic choices.

You may want to paint different scenarios and find out what different impacts they would have. You could project into the future and see how each scenario will look. The best way to know is to draw a matrix for each scenario and see if you move significantly. Keep in mind, you can control the left to right movement across the business strength axis, but external factors are controlling the industry attractive axis. That is important because you may decide to improve your position by investing in an area that will move the SBU to the left. But if your analysis shows that the SBU is going down because of a negative external factor, that would be an indication that it is not a good approach.

Summary

In this chapter we discussed two new techniques which can help us develop exciting and creative strategies. Those techniques include the Boston Consulting Group Matrix and the Nine-Cell Business Strength/Industry Attractiveness Matrix. These matrixes differ from financial models in that they consider synergy. They also provide us with more specifics for both allocation choices and competitive possibilities. They really help us pick the appropriate paints from our palette. In addition, we also projected the nine-cell matrix into the future, changing the industry attractiveness weights and the business strength criteria. This allowed us to review the importance of the industry in the future and determine the impact of our strategic choices.

Now, utilizing everything we have developed so far, you should really be ready to do some serious creative painting. First you developed your pallet, next you found out about your skills and desires, and then looked at what others had done. Then, using financial modeling, you sketched in your outline, filling it in with information gleaned from the experience curve and product life cycle, putting it all together using portfolio models. Now you have the "how." It's time to determine the "when" and "where."

Chapter 7

Making it Happen:
Implementation Planning

When you are starting to paint, you have your palette set, you know what you want to accomplish, and you are familiar with all the tools, you might say that you have the "how" ready. Now it is time to develop the "where" and "when." We are not painting at this stage, we are preparing a list to make sure that everything is in order to paint. Strategic planners call this implementation planning.

Implementation is a very important part of the strategic planning process. Even though you may be a competent strategic plan developer, if you do not know how to implement effectively, the probability of success is significantly diminished. A good strategic plan implemented effectively almost always achieves a relatively high degree of success. A good strategic plan implemented poorly typically generates less than desirable results, and can often lead to a disaster. But even a mediocre strategic plan that is implemented effectively can routinely achieve a satisfactory level of success.

Remember, implementation planning is one of several phases in the strategic planning process. The first phase in the process is the development of the organization's mission. The second phase involves the definition of the organization's goals and objectives. Phase three encompasses external and internal environmental scanning, which is followed by phase four, strategy formulation. After strategy formulation, implementation planning, which is the fifth phase of the process, is considered. The final phase is the development of a control mechanism to monitor the process and provide feedback information on the actual status and progress accomplishments.

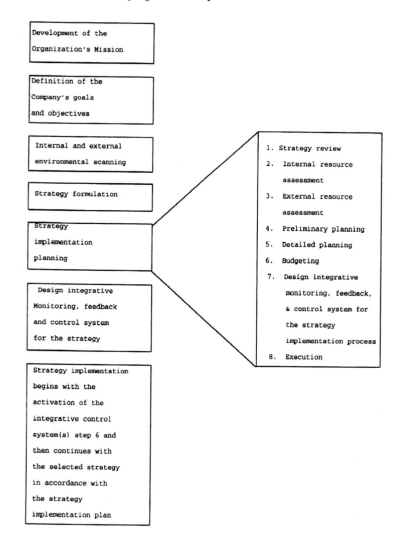

Strategic Planning-Implementation Planning Process
Figure 7.1

The focus of this chapter is on the implementation-planning phase of the strategic planning process, which is depicted in Figure 7.1. Implementation planning is a process within a process where each component is linked together via feedback.

Methodology for Strategy Implementation Planning

The proposed Methodology for Strategy Implementation Planning (MSIP) is *not* the actual implementation. MSIP is a procedure for planning the implementation. The strategic plan is not actually implemented at this point of the strategic planning process. Actual implementation does not begin until after the strategic planning monitoring and control system(s) are in place. The proposed Methodology for Strategy Implementation Planning consists of the following eight steps and an integrative monitoring, feedback, and control process. The proposed methodology is illustrated in the Figure 7.2.

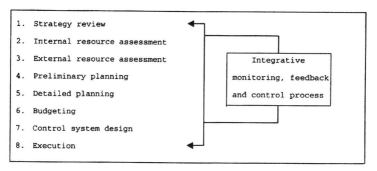

A Methodology for Strategic Implementation Planning (MSIP)
Figure 7.2

If this looks familiar, it should, since it is basically the same format that is employed in traditional strategic planning procedures. However, even though the process may look similar, the concerns as they relate to strategy implementation are very different.

Phase 1: Strategy Review

Strategy review is concerned with trying to obtain an overall picture of the strategy. The questions of how the strategy is going to affect the overall organization and who within the organization are going to be most affected should be addressed at this time. For example, the implementation planner may ask questions such as: Is this strategy encompassing one particular functional area of an SBU or the entire SBU?

Also, it is important to understand the implications of the strategy within the organization as a whole. Therefore, the implementor has to understand the objectives of the strategy in relation to the organization's objectives. In this context, it is important to know the mission of the organization, its goals and objectives, and how the strategy matches the organization's personality. The implementor needs to ask questions such as: Is this strategy in line with the organization's mission? Is it helping to achieve the organization's goals and objectives? In effect, the implementor has to understand the objectives of the strategy, why it was selected and its impact on the organization as it exists in its current form. Once we have an overall picture and understand the implications of the strategy in the context of the organization's mission and objectives, we need to seek information about the organization's capabilities as well as the existence of external factors that could facilitate the implementation of our strategy.

Phase 2: Internal Resource Assessment

Internal resource assessment is concerned with three aspects of the SBU. First, it looks at each functional area of the SBU. Next, it looks at the organization as a whole, and then at the human capabilities of the organization. In other words, what capabilities does the organization possess internally that will aid in making our strategy work?

Functional Resources

Functional assessment describes the means or methods that are to be used by each of the functional areas of the SBU in carrying out the allocation and/or competitive strategy. Internal resource assessment of the SBU entails reviewing the capabilities available to us in the

SBU's functional areas such as marketing, production/operations, research and development, human resource management, finance, and information systems, in relation to their capabilities, limitations and uniqueness. For example:

Marketing

In marketing, each aspect of the marketing mix (product, price, promotion, and distribution) must be analyzed in order to determine if any changes need to be made to facilitate the implementation of a particular strategy. The SBU's product line and product packaging must be analyzed in relation to its strengths and weaknesses and the possible effects if new products are introduced. For example, if our new strategy was to develop international markets, it might be necessary to change our product so that it conforms to differing national tastes. Current pricing strategies need to be studied to determine if any change is required to implement a certain strategy. Also, the SBU's promotion expertise should be analyzed to determine its capabilities and limitations with respect to the implementation of a particular strategy.

Production/Operations

Assessment in the production/operations area includes plant capabilities, which entails plant size, capacity, and present utilization. The current method of manufacturing and its capabilities must be understood when implementing a strategy. It should be determined how production could be manipulated in order to effectively carry out a strategy. If, for example, we were going to develop an e-commerce initiative, we might need to modify our production capabilities to be more responsive to individual requests.

Research and Development

Assessment in the research and development area includes listing all of the company's research capabilities including type, quantity and quality of researchers, research facilities, and current research expertise.

Personnel/Human Resource Management

Personnel/Human Resource Management is a significant part of the strategic implementation planning process although its importance has often been understated. Issues of concern here are staffing and perhaps even more important, training. When a new strategy is implemented, it often requires new people and/or extensive training of new and/or existing employees. The organization's prior policy regarding promoting from within and training must be reviewed.

Finance

The financial functional area assessment includes the financial resources available to the SBU, cash handling procedures, and cash flow capabilities. Attention should also be given to audit and accounting capabilities. Normally, a new strategy or problem solution would require some outlay of funds. We need to know how available these funds are.

Information Systems

Information has really not been recognized as a strategic resource until relatively recently. Because of e-business, information systems are becoming a very important area in the internal resource assessment. These systems are also a vital part of the implementation process because they are often central components of the control process.

It is evident that an in-depth analysis of all of the functional areas of the company is of vital importance as part of the internal resource assessment.

SBU Organizational Resources

Organizationally, we focus on the structure, culture, and communication aspects of the SBU in terms of their capabilities, limitations and/or uniqueness. In other words, we are viewing our SBUs from a macro perspective as part of the internal resource assessment.

In this respect, one issue to consider is matching strategy to organizational structure. Considerable research has been conducted on the relationship between organizational structure and strategy. Generally, it has been found that strategy and structure must be properly aligned if the organization is to be successful in achieving its objectives and that an organization can seldom deviate substantially from its current strategy without major alterations in its structure.

Organizational culture is the pattern of beliefs and expectations shared by the organization's members who influence the behavior of individuals and groups within the organization. Organizational culture could be crucial in establishing organizational SBU, and therefore, must be thoroughly understood.

Phase 3: External Resource Assessment

The third phase in the proposed MSIP is external resource assessment. Earlier under the internal assessment phase, we set out to determine the resources the organization has that will facilitate carrying out the particular strategy that has been chosen. In the external resource assessment, it is time to determine what elements in the external environment can facilitate or hinder the implementation process. External resource assessment includes a review of external elements including the political environment, the legal environment, economic conditions, the current level and the rate of change of technology, and social issues that could affect the implementation process. It should be clear that these elements are being reviewed with a different perspective than they were in the strategic planning process. These external factors are now reviewed on the basis of how they could affect the implementation process. For example, a review of the legal environment might concern itself with the possibility of a problem or benefit due to a particular local ordinance or federal law. For instance, a firm which decides to construct a new facility as part of its implementation plan would like to have a good understanding of all the local ordinances relating to zoning, noise and pollution. Additionally, the facility would also have to conform to statutes enforced by federal agencies such as the EPA, the EEOC, OSHA, etc. In contrast, when external factors are reviewed under the environmental scanning step in the strategic planning process, the purpose is to see if the organization's strategy could be impacted by any legal constraints such as liability issues and federal laws.

Phase 4: Preliminary Planning

The fourth phase in the implementation process is the preliminary planning stage. This stage directly affects the success of the detailed planning phase, and therefore is a vital part of the implementation methodology. The first step in preliminary planning is referred to as the work breakdown process. In this step the overall effort required to implement the strategy is repeatedly subdivided into smaller and smaller "chunks" until a manageable level of work is obtained. In general, the implementation of a strategy would be classified as a program. During the work breakdown process this program would be subdivided into projects, the projects would be subdivided into subprojects, the subprojects would then be divided into work packages, and the work packages would be divided into tasks or activities. Five levels of disaggregation are often enough for small and medium sized programs. For larger efforts, tasks can be further subdivided into subtasks and, if necessary, subtasks can be subdivided into work elements. Rarely is there a need to go beyond seven levels in the work breakdown process. Once the subdivision of effort is complete, it is necessary to obtain estimates of the time and cost to accomplish each task, and to specify the resources required. This information is most often obtained from the individual or group responsible for performing the task. The output from the work breakdown process is referred to as a task list. A task list consists of a listing for each task, which includes a description of the work to be done and/or the result(s), the estimated time, the estimated cost, and the resources necessary to accomplish the task.

The next step in the preliminary planning process is the comparison of the resource requirements specified in the task list with the internal and external resource assessments. The purpose of this step is to determine what required resources are not currently available within the organization, and how and when these resources would be acquired. For example, if part of implementing a strategy requires acquiring a building, then the process of deciding whether to buy, lease, or build a facility should begin at this time.

Phase 5: Detailed Planning

The fifth phase of the proposed methodology for Strategy Implementation Planning is the development of the actual implementation plan. Project management techniques are often employed at this stage. The most popular methods are the Critical Path Method (CPM) and the Program Evaluation and Review Techniques (PERT). Both PERT and CPM are based on a network model of the project. Information from the task list generated by the work breakdown process is utilized to construct the network model. The model depicts the tasks required to accomplish the project and the precedence relationships among the tasks. The precedence relationships are typically specified as part of the work breakdown process.

Once the model is complete, the analysis of the model can begin. The analysis of the model generates information that is extremely useful to the project manager or strategy implementor in managing the associated project. Both PERT and CPM analyses generate estimates of the earliest start time, the latest completion time, and the amount of slack for each task. Simulation is often used in conjunction with multiple estimates of task durations in PERT to provide probabilistic estimates of project task times. The earliest start time and latest completion time provide the project scheduler with an "execution window" within which the task must be accomplished. Slack is a measure of the flexibility in scheduling a task, meaning the less slack, the less scheduling flexibility. From a scheduling perspective, tasks with the least slack are the most critical with respect to on-time project completion.

Gantt Charts are also often used by project managers or strategy implementers to graphically illustrate the results of project network analysis. A Gantt Chart lists all of the project's tasks in order, from top to bottom on the vertical axis. Time is the variable on the horizontal axis. Time periods indicated on the time axis can be days, weeks, or months. The length of time for each task is then shown as a horizontal dark line. The start and stop times are indicated by where the line starts and stops (Figure 7.3). Gantt Charts are simple yet effective ways of looking at a project.

Once actual scheduling decisions have been made, the network models can be adjusted and re-analyzed to assist project planners in developing a project budget. The network model can also be very useful in the control phase of project management. As tasks are started and completed, actual times and costs can be substituted for the estimates from the original analysis. Then, by re-analyzing the network model the project manager can obtain information that will indicate whether or not actual progress is in accordance with the planned implementation schedule.

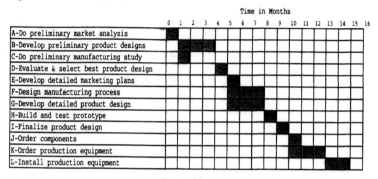

Gantt Chart
Figure 7.3

Phase 6: Budgeting

Budgeting is the sixth phase of the implementation methodology. It seems to have gained some recognition recently, since several authors are now referring to it in their discussions about implementation. This recognition of budgetary importance has likely been inspired by the overwhelming mass of data that shows that implementation failures are often caused by insufficient and inadequate funding.

However, the budgeting process can be made much simpler and more effective if the implementor has followed the MSIP approach to implementation. A good Work Breakdown Schedule (WBS) divides the implementation plan into many smaller manageable components that can be accumulated into one master budget. Obviously, the total budget is the sum of each of its smaller elements. When one activity incurs a cost overrun, the impact is simultaneously felt in the total project budget.

Make-or-buy decisions, which are typically controlling/comptrolling activities, occur during the implementation process. In most cases, when strategies call for significant changes in the corporation, rarely is there such an abundance of funds that trade-off decisions can be ignored. This type of decision comes into play in all parts of the implementation plan. For example, in the area of staffing, the question may be related to the training process. Does the company hire its own training group or is that left to outsiders? The most direct and obvious area of make-or-buy decisions is that of capital expenditures. Very often strategies require additional production facilities and equipment. A decision whether to lease, buy, or build has to be made. Often a combination of the above is the appropriate decision. In any case, the process is simplified through the use of the WBS since each element can be scrutinized closely.

Because the timing of each activity has been delineated, the problem of determining when cash has to be injected into the process can easily be resolved. Many strategic plans would not be implementable if all of the required funds had to be allocated on day one of the implementation process. The strategic implementation process allows for systematic cash handling and, as exemplified in the management of business operations, cash flow must be watched very closely in all phases of the business, including the implementation process.

Phase 7: Control System Design

The design of control systems is concerned with the determination of WHAT data/information should be gathered, HOW this data/information should be gathered (forms, methods, etc.), and WHEN (frequency) or WHERE (at what point in the process) this data/information should be gathered. Consideration must also be given to the WHAT, HOW and WHEN of reporting the data/information gathered in the monitoring process.

Control systems design also requires that specific standards of performance be established. These standards must be quantifiable and measurable to be useful as control elements. However, since implementation is so dynamic, consideration must be given to the possible variability of the performance measurements. Therefore, a certain degree of tolerance should be incorporated when establishing these standards. In other words, it would be more effective to provide an acceptable range of values as a standard versus one specific point.

Monitoring, feedback, and control is also an integrative process that links all of the phases in the implementation process together. It is a critical aspect of the methodology. Since implementation is a dynamic process, which is taking place in a dynamic environment, the monitoring process must start with the review of the external and internal environment and continue through to execution.

All too often organizations develop criteria for evaluation and evaluate performance but do not follow up with appropriate actions. All of the phases in the implementation methodology are of little value if feedback is not provided to the appropriate managers and any necessary corrective action is not taken. Of course, no corrective action may be necessary if performance criteria are being met in a satisfactory manner. Common causes of deviation from acceptable standards include:

- Unrealistic objectives
- Selection of the wrong strategy to achieve organizational objectives
- Use of the wrong organizational structure to implement the strategy
- Ineptness or negligence on the part of management and/or employees
- Lack of motivation
- Lack of communication with the organization
- Environmental forces

If performance criteria are not being met satisfactorily, management must investigate, find the cause of the deviation, and correct it. The monitoring and reporting of actual progress (feedback) is a critical element in the strategic implementation process.

Phase 8: Execution

The final phase in the implementation methodology involves deciding how we are going to implement the strategy. There are two primary ways of executing a strategy: (1) a one-step approach or (2) a phased approach. A one-step process means that the strategy is executed all at once. For example, if the strategic plan involves increasing the quality of a product, once the desired level of quality has been reached, the strategy is accomplished and the process is considered complete.

In the phased execution approach, parts of the strategy are executed one at a time until the whole plan is completed. The phased execution approach is more often utilized in conjunction with longer and more complex strategies where the completion of the strategy depends upon the sequential completion of phases.

When deciding which approach is to be used, certain factors uncovered in the internal and external environmental scanning phases should be considered. Strategies that are executed using the one-step approach are generally short-lived. Also, strategies that are capable of being implemented all at once are usually less time consuming, and often deal with a trendy product or result from emergency situations.

An example of a one-step approach was Johnson and Johnson's strategy to overcome the negative publicity surrounding the Tylenol product tampering case. Just prior to the poisoning tragedy involving Tylenol, Johnson and Johnson's per share stock price had risen from the low 20's to the high 40's. After the incident, which investigators felt was product tampering, the company experienced a tremendous increase in costs related to lost sales, repackaging, and product recall. Early in the crisis, management sprang into action. First, Johnson and Johnson recalled approximately 100,000 bottles of Tylenol from locations scattered across the country. Then, the firm sent telegrams to doctors, hospitals, and distributors at a cost of approximately $500,000. All advertising for Tylenol was immediately suspended. Then Johnson and Johnson notified the FDA and the media and set up an emergency hot-line to answer questions from consumers and health care professionals. It also offered a reward for information leading to the arrest and conviction of persons responsible for the tampering.

Then Johnson and Johnson immediately began planning its comeback. The strategy committee met twice daily for six weeks and dealt with every issue from packaging to advertising to appearances on television. Although many had doubts as to whether Johnson and Johnson would ever recover its earlier position, Tylenol regained over 65% of its sales within a year of the incident. Obviously, this kind of emergency has to utilize an implementation plan that is executed immediately.

Strategies that are executed in phases generally involve large or significant changes. They are typically more complex strategies and involve different or multiple units within the organization performing segments of the implementation plan at different times. An example of a phased implementation approach would be the sequential or phased closing down and/or selling off of several operating units that were not considered part of the core business by a large company that had decided on a contraction strategy. They are likely to implement their strategy in phases in order to minimize the impact on cash flow.

Why MSIP?

As discussed earlier, traditional approaches to strategy implementation are limited in that they do not provide a definitive step-by-step procedure. The proposed Methodology for Strategy Implementation Planning (MSIP) is a pragmatic step-by-step approach

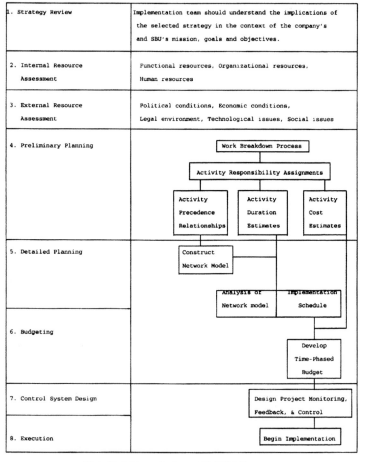

Detailed Description of MSIP Process
Figure 7.4

to implementation. With this system, those involved with the implementation will not only "see" the issues, but will also perceive how the phases of the process are dependent upon one another, and gain a sense of the timing that should come into play. Figure 7.4 presents a detailed outline of the MSIP process.

The benefits provided by a pragmatic methodology for strategy implementation planning are numerous. First, it forces the planner to scrutinize each elemental part of the organization and determine if the organization's strategic plan is feasible. Long before the organization actually starts spending on the actual implementation, it allows for a determination of the practicality of the process. Second, strategic planning is a dynamic process. Once the strategic plan is developed, the monitoring and control system is activated and then the strategy is implemented. However, since strategic planning always involves a continual review of the external environment, an unexpected obstacle may present itself, which could result in a decision to change the strategy. The methodology provides for this contingency and allows the strategy and the corresponding plan to be changed in mid-stream, if this action is warranted. It also provides the strategic planner with an idea of what the costs would be to change strategies. Therefore, a more realistic decision can be made as to the true cost and value of changing strategies in mid-stream. In other words, if you want to change to a strategy that will increase your profits by 1 million dollars, but the cost of changing it would be 1.5 million dollars, you might not want to do it even though at first it seemed like a good idea.

Participation in the Implementation Process

The implementation methodology discussed above is an effective, pragmatic procedure for implementing a strategy. This methodology, however, is not an automated process. We cannot push a button to cause it to happen, or execute the MSIP program on a computer. It is a framework or set of procedures, that guides people through the process of implementing a strategic plan. Human judgement and creativity are required in every phase. Implementing a strategy can be and often is one of the broadest activities that occurs in an organization. Every area of the organization can be involved and/or affected. Therefore, in order for it to be effective, every person in the organization should be involved at some level in the strategy implementation planning process.

Summary

Although implementation is a very important part of strategic planning, not much attention has been paid to it. However, a well thought out strategy has little value unless it is effectively implemented. To this end a strategy implementation planning process is invaluable.

The implementation of a strategy can be described and conducted as a project. With this in mind, a project management-based procedure has been presented. The object being to assemble the important issues in strategy implementation planning so that you can not only "see" the necessary steps for successful strategy implementation, but also perceive how each is dependent upon the others and provides a sense of the timing that comes into play as the implementation process develops. The process presented, a methodology for strategy implementation planning (MSIP), contains the following steps: (1) strategy review, (2) internal resource assessment, (3) external resource assessment, (4) preliminary planning, (5) detailed planning, (6) budgeting, (7) control system design, (8) execution, and an integrative monitoring, feedback and control process.

In addition, since every area of the entire organization and its SBUs is often affected by each SBU's strategy, and since strategy must receive support from both the SBUs and the other company's members, it is important that every person in the organization be involved at some level in the strategy implementation planning process.

Now that we know the "how" from the previous chapters and the "when" and "where" from this chapter we are almost ready to paint our strategic masterpiece. But there is still one more issue of concern. The one step yet to be developed is a way to constantly check our progress to see if we are on the right track, and if not, to quickly and simply make the needed corrections. That step is called monitoring and controlling and it is the subject of the final chapter.

Chapter 8

Checking Your Work:
Monitoring and Control

Up to this point most of the elements of painting have been discussed. A method of categorizing our paints which utilizes all of the basic colors and allows us to take advantage of all of the possible combinations of colors has been developed, and those paints have been placed on our palette in a systematic manner. We then defined our capabilities and decided what we wanted to paint and how we were going to express our own ideas. Next we looked at mixing colors and then picking the right ones appropriate for what we were trying to accomplish. We have laid out our ideas in a manner that can let our creativity guide us to make that masterpiece. Using the approach presented in this book you hopefully came to understand that, with a little luck thrown in, you too can start to create like the masters. Now put on the blindfold and go to it. No? Does it seem silly that you should paint with a blindfold on?

Running an organization without effective controls is just like painting with a blindfold. You are only successful if you are very lucky. Even though controlling is the last step in the strategic planning process it plays an important part with each step before it. Control closes the loop in the planning process providing valuable information and allowing you to constantly adjust your approach.

Controlling consists of the methods and mechanisms that managers use to ensure that behaviors and performances conform to the organization's goals and objectives. In other words, it is the way that management checks what the organization is doing and compares that with the goals and objectives set forth in the strategic plan. Then, if there is a problem, management can make changes early, preventing serious and often more costly problems. It is always easier to make small continuous changes than to completely change an organization's direction.

Controlling has been defined as the process of monitoring performance and taking action to ensure the desired results. Its purpose is to make sure that the actual performance is consistent with the plan. The focus of control is on preventing problems, correcting problems, and exploring opportunities.

The control formula is:

Need for Action = Desired Performance – Actual Performance
(NFA = DP – AP)

When actual performance is less than desired performance, a need for corrective action exists. When actual performance is greater than desired, a need exists to determine why, in order to ensure that the high level of accomplishment can be maintained in the future, or to re-evaluate standards to determine if they should be revised.

Some of the forces that create the need for control have been identified as uncertainty, complexity, human limitations, and delegation and decentralization. Uncertainty exists because plans and objectives deal with the uncertain future, defined when we projected our environmental scan. Control allows for constructive adjustments. Complexity requires that activities be coordinated and integrated. Rapidly changing and unpredictable environments highlight the human limitations of judgement and forecasting, and control identifies the errors that can occur. Control mechanisms aid in the delegation and decentralization of decision-making authority. As the authority to act moves down the hierarchy of control, control mechanisms ensure that accountability flows back up.

Controlling is a lot different from what most people think it is. When the word control is mentioned an image of some medieval dungeon pops immediately into our heads, or that big brother is watching us, ready to punish at the drop of a hat.

It is true that some companies do control situations through the use of cameras and video equipment. For example, have you ever walked into a casino? From the first moment you walk into the gambling floor you are being watched. Primarily these devices are installed to keep the games honest, but they also warn casino owners of potential problems.

However, there are other less intrusive methods that can be utilized for organizational control. In the past several years Wal-Mart stores have grown in record numbers. Using computer technology, managers and store employees talk to each other face-to-face via satellite and video monitors. Computers also help Wal-Mart keep a record of sales and inventory so that managers know exactly what is happening in the stores, and can track up to 30,000 products at the touch of a button. The computer tells when a particular product is ordered from a vendor, where it is in the distribution channel, and when the actual sale is made to the customer. This has kept the costs down so that Wal-Mart can pass the savings on to the customer. But that is not where the story ends.

Unlike the intimidating big-brother approach, Wal-Mart has found that they did not have to "brow beat" their associates, instead they control themselves. Each employee is encouraged to be part of the process. If they see a way to get the job done better, they are encouraged to bring the idea up at anytime. What is so unique is that managers actually do listen and act on the suggestions. By developing a close relationship with its employees, Wal-Mart has developed a "family," and the positive effects on performance speak for themselves.

Where to Control?

Often times, controlling the simplest of things yields the best results. Take for instance the airlines. Before every plane lifts off the ground, or even leaves the gate, each crew goes through a checklist to ensure that the plane is ready for flight. Proper use of the checklist ensures that all of the critical items are operating correctly and set in their proper position. If they did not use such measures they might get caught with a surprise in mid-flight. Managers have to find areas that might cause problems or have the highest potential for problems.

Another example is the automobile. Controls are placed in the form of gauges, in areas where the highest potential for problems can occur, such as oil levels and water temperature. If left unchecked these areas can be very detrimental to the operation of the car. That is why we control them.

When you are not sure where to place your controls, there is a temptation to place them everywhere. However, too much control can be detrimental as well. You can imagine how long it would take to get an airplane into flight if the checklist covered every item on the plane.

In terms of the organization, managers might consider placing controls in production rather than in R&D, unless, of course, R&D takes particular precedence over production. Keep the level of control isolated to only the most important areas. Where is control most needed? In general, the answer is, like the airplane, in the most critical areas.

Critical success areas vary from industry to industry. The fashion industry values secrecy higher than anything when a new line comes out. The uniqueness of the line, those things that differentiate it from all others, must be guarded above all else. To maintain tight secrecy garment designers go to great lengths. That's a form of control. Critical success areas are any area that is vital to the success of your organization. Maintaining high levels of control ensures the long-term viability of an organization.

All of these areas fall primarily into two types of controls: preventive and corrective. Preventive controls are those things that we use to limit the chance for error such as rules, guidelines, and procedures. Of course none of this matters if an organization does not have trained individuals motivated to getting the job done right. If the airlines employed individuals who did not pay attention to details and were not well trained, air travel would be a very dangerous form of transportation.

The idea is if we do the job right the first time, the way it was meant to be done, we limit the costs and increase the quality of the job performed. Therefore, the preventive controls should be designed to achieve the goals and objectives of the organization. This only happens if the workforce adheres to the restrictions and limits placed upon it.

The second type of control is corrective control. Corrective controls are the means by which managers have to fix unwanted practices or procedures. Through corrective controls, managers can correct problems in shipping, distribution, inventory levels, and the like. Correcting a problem before a major situation happens can save the organization a lot of time, money, and manpower.

How to Manage the Control Process

There is a generally accepted method to control an organization. This method is straightforward and is very important to the understanding of controlling.

The control process consists of a six-step process:

1)   Determine what to control.
2)   Set control standards.
3)   Measure performance.
4)   Compare performance to standards.
5)   Determine reasons for deviations.
6)   Take corrective actions.

Determine What To Control

Let's go back to the painting scenario. We know that we can not paint effectively with a blindfold on. So how do we manage the images of our painting so that they represent what we have set out to paint? We place lines on the canvas so that each line connects together with other lines so that when joined the lines look like our subject. We constantly judge our own performance and adjust shading and shapes to make them more representative. Just like shading and shapes, controlling a process can create the correct output desired by the strategic plan. What we control is very important.

Management control measures the success of individual units in an organization, maintaining prescribed level issues by the strategic plan. (For example, are budgets being followed?) This type of control can utilize financial ratios. Some of these have been discussed in Chapter 4. Operational control measures the individual performance of units or individuals (i.e., are quotas being met?). There is a fine line between each of these measures and often one gets mistaken for the other.

When considering what to control operationally, managers should keep in mind the processes that are used. How a product or service is produced can give many clues as to what you should control. A fairly new concept used to determine the most important areas to look at when setting up a control system is called process mapping. Process mapping consist of laying out a linear flow chart of all of the activities involved in producing a product or providing a service. A process map of a production system would include everything from ordering the raw materials to inventorying them to each of the processes that are used in production to shipping. Process mapping illustrates not only the specific tasks, but also their interrelationships. By checking this flow chart, one can more easily get a picture of what controls are needed.

Performance factors are of particular importance and should be part of the control system for each area where a job is performed.

Performance factors come in two varieties, people and things. When considering how to control, managers need to consider the following:

1) Quantity
2) Quality
3) Time
4) Cost

By manipulating these four areas, managers can limit performance factors and maintain positive control. A goal for controlling can be to maintain the highest quantity with the highest quality in the shortest time while keeping costs as low as possible.

Be aware that there are problems when considering what information you are using when controlling. Often when managers look at information being measured they sometimes forget that the information may not be relevant until it is compared to the objectives. Consider that you are interested in reaching certain levels of production in your manufacturing facility. In order to ensure that your output will meet your goals, you send a team into the shop to make sure all is well. After a few days, your team reports back saying that it appears as though your plant workers are not motivated, since they do a lot of standing around. Accordingly, you develop a motivation program to address the issue. Although this will be an expensive and time-consuming program, you feel it will make the difference in meeting your production goals. After the program is in place, you check your output and you still are not on schedule to make your goals. What has gone wrong? After rechecking, you learn that there is poor communication between inventory control and production. The reason why everyone was standing around was not that they were poorly motivated, it was because they were waiting for materials. It was an expensive lesson, but you learned to not look at what is occurring in only one control measure, rather to look at the entire process.

Another problematic area of concern when looking at control measures is conflicting control measures, such as trying to increase sales while cutting costs in the sales staff. Sub-optimization is a problem facing many large organizations today because they have lost the big picture. If management wants to increase efficiency in the organization then it must consider all consequences of control.

Set Control Standards

Once management has figured out what to control it needs to set standards by which performance can be measured. This is necessary because without standards, management has nothing to judge or measure against. In the control formula, $NFA = DP - AP$, this is the DP (Desired Performance).

It is very important at this stage that the standards set be very concise and specific. Managerial standards are usually goals and objectives set in the strategic planning process, while operational standards are the "hurdles" necessary to meet those managerial standards. If the standards are not well defined it might be important to go back and redefine the original goals. If goals and objective are too general they can not be accurately used as standards because they do not give correct levels of measurement when needed.

Sometimes goals and objectives are just not well defined. For example, when setting a specific level of responsibility, managers use what is called a surrogate standard. A surrogate standard is a related issue which has very little to do with the standard being set. For example, if a university wanted to increase the image it projects to the community where it is located, it might measure the number of hours spent by students in community service. Increasing the amount of hours spent in community service increases the awareness of the community about the university. More hours make for higher awareness. The greater awareness, the better the image. All things come together to give a reliable measure of the standard.

Another type of standard is the tolerance standard. There may be a time when a standard will need to be within a certain range for acceptance. Let's say one out of every three students should do community service. By allowing a deviance managers allow for those unforeseen circumstances. Tolerance limits set boundaries by which deviations can occur and still be considered acceptable.

Measure Performance

Management has decided what to measure and set the limits by which it will be measured; it is now time to discuss how to measure the performance of an action. In the control formula $NFA = DP - AP$, this is the AP (Actual Performance).

Access to appropriate and timely information is needed to measure and evaluate performance. Measuring performance relies heavily on the information gathered though management information systems, feedback, and comments by customers. It is easy to see how managers can get overloaded with a deluge of information, so it is best to have an idea of what information is required before beginning to measure.

Here are some guidelines that might help limit the amount of information received.

> 1. Report only the information needed to develop a reliable picture of performance. Excess information raises costs unnecessarily.
> 2. Isolate information to only what is strategically important information.
> 3. Report only important information. Keep the report lean. Reaction to a problem area can be crucial and if there is too much information what is important can be hidden away.
> 4. Prepare reports so that they are timely, but not too often   as this often clouds the issue.
> 5. Tailor reports so that only necessary information is routed to managers. If it does not concern them don't give it to them.
> 6. Use reports so that they announce problem areas first then inform.

When information is presented in this way managers have information they can use to correct problems should they arise. It also presents the manager the opportunity to correct what's wrong before it becomes a major issue.

Another means of measuring performance is through the use of budgets. Budgets provide a quick measuring tool for the manager.

Keeping a project or organization on budget is as important as the performance action itself. This does not necessarily mean that the best action should be the least costly. Instead it should be the goal of managers to use the money in a budget the best way possible with as little waste possible.

The type of technique used to measure performance varies with the type of performance factor being measured. Each manager must know the type of performance factor they wish to measure. Some types of measurements include: market oriented, human resources, production, and audits.

The following are some of the ways to measure an organization in the market place.

1. Sales analysis compares projected sales with actual sales. This method has limits in that sales goals are often distorted. Price and volume fluctuate regularly and can have a disastrous effect on sales.
2. Marketing expenses to sales ratios let an organization know if it is over spending to achieve its market share.
3. Market share compares sales in an industry compared to others in the market (competitors). It looks at the areas of basic market share (how much?), amount of target audience reached, and relative market share, which we talked about in Chapter 5.
4. Customer response lets us know how the customer feels about the product.
5. Is the organization producing efficiently? Efficiency analysis controls the costs of the sales force, distribution system, and advertising.

Here are some of the ways to measure human resource performance.

1. Evaluate the quality and quantity of the product that a particular worker is producing.
2. Performance appraisals are used to accomplish two primary functions. First, it gives the organization a yardstick to indicate those employees who set themselves above the norm. This information can be used for raises, promotions, and gifts. Second, it allows employees to strive to improve for tomorrow.

The organization also benefits because the work force is more motivated, has a better attitude toward managerial decisions, has an increased desire to learn and train, and it reduces the opportunity to play favorites.

There are primarily three types of production measures. Inputs, or precontrol methods, limit capital resources so that each resource is used when it is needed. Precontrol methods tell how much of a resource will be needed to accomplish a particular job. Inventory control is a good example of this. "Just-in-time" inventory requirements use resources as they are needed limiting excess inventory at the process sight.

The second method is concurrent control. Concurrent control, often referred to as production scheduling, employs network models such as PERT/CPM. PERT or Program Evaluation and Review Technique, is a network model designed to maximize efficient movement of a project through a plant. PERT/CPM was discussed in implementation planning (Chapter 7).

Postcontrol actually measures the output. By using postcontrol measures, managers can increase the reliability of the project and the efficiency of the output. There are several postcontrol methods. One is standard cost analysis, where managers add up the actual per unit costs and compare them with a standard cost per unit. If there are any differences, those differences must be explained. Checking each item as it comes off the production line is another. This is very costly and is often now done only for major projects. In most cases, statistical quality control is now used. It limits the amount of defective units being shipped, because the outputs of the line are compared to a "statistical unit." This method lowers the time and money necessary to maintain an acceptable level of quality.

Control also uses audits. Audits allow for periodical review of a process. An audit systematically checks all parts associated with a process. It helps to lessen the error factors by finding them before they become too large. Audits can be narrow in scope, such as a vertical audit, which would be used for an in-depth analysis of one specific component, or they can be very broad. A horizontal audit evaluates the entire operation of a particular function. Be they vertical or horizontal, audits often focus of specific areas of concern.

Management audits look at the performance of the management team. Specifically, how effective has the team managed the objectives of the organization? Have the policies to achieve the organization's objectives been effective? It is often important to look into these areas, because sometimes if the process is not governed well, no matter how good controls are, there still could be problems.

Financial audits utilize the financial information generated by the organization. Here is where budgets become important. As a control method, budgets provide a quick indication when something is going wrong. Keeping within a budget is important. Auditing the budget tells where problems might exist.

Social Performance audits measure the performance of an organization from the perspective of its stakeholder. This type of audit defines how the organization is living up to the social performance expectations of its stakeholders.

Remember to be careful when measuring performance. Often what you are measuring may not provide the information that you require. You may be trying to measure salesforce performance by comparing last year's sales to this year's sales. Seeing a drop, you might assume that the salesforce is not performing as well as they have in the past. However, the problem is not with the salesforce. In this case, production has slowed down and the salesforce could obviously not sell what they did not have.

One last problem with measuring performance is that it is often time consuming, costly, and may not always be possible. If not, find some way to get the information. There is a world of possibilities - just look for them.

Compare Performance to Standards

Comparing standards and performance requires that the same terms used for setting the standards and for measuring performance. Setting standards and measuring performance are two separate activities and there is no benefit derived from their analyses unless they are compared. When management compares performance against standards they get a measurement of how a process is doing. It is most important however, to allow the data to stand alone. Compare what is happening to what is expected to happen.

Determine Reasons for Deviations

Very often, young inexperienced business people and newly hired executives go into a business that appears to have some problems and immediately start to make changes. Either they are simply very enthusiastic and want to move quickly or perhaps they just want to put their mark on the company. However, it often turns out to be a big mistake. Making changes to a company can be a very destructive process, and making changes that are not necessary can be even more destructive. Therefore, determining the reasons for deviation is one of the more important elements of the control process. A thorough analysis of why deviations occur is a vital and necessary step that can form the foundation for proper corrective action. Deviations from standards do not always signify the existence of a performance problem. Many standards are interrelated and the effects of poor performance of one can often be minimized by the positive performance of another. The related standards have to be examined to make sure that a problem actually exists.

Certain questions need to be asked:

1. Are the standards appropriate for what is being measured?
2. Are there external factors that are affecting the standards making them inappropriate?
3. Is the strategy that is the basis for the measurement standards appropriate?
4. Are the activities being performed appropriate for achieving the standard?
5. Is the organizational support necessary to achieve the strategy in place?

Take Corrective Actions

Once there is conclusive evidence that a problem exists, it becomes appropriate to take corrective actions. Corrective actions are exemplified in the feedback loop of the strategic planning process. Since monitoring is done during all stages of the strategic planning process then corrective action can take place at any time and in any stage. You may find, for example, that you are unable to meet the certain goals set forth in the strategic plan because the limits of the mission statement do not allow you to focus in an area relevant to the goal. For example, your mission statement says that your customers are "large businesses." Yet your goals call for sales that are so high that the constraint of selling only to "large businesses" holds you back. You must, therefore, go back and change your mission statement, or realizing that there is a good reason for the "large business" constraint in the mission statement, change your goal.

In addition to the possibility of changing areas of the strategic plan, it may also be necessary to modify the creative approach that you have selected as part of your strategy. You may have elected to implement a new promotional campaign as part of your strategic plan, and that particular campaign has not provided the desired results. The idea of developing a new promotional campaign may still be the best course of action, but you may need a different approach.

Also, because of the interrelationships that exist in the above areas, an adjustment in one may require an adjustment in another area. A strategy to establish a market overseas would require adjustments in structure, systems, and resource support.

Control Systems

The purpose of the control system is to ensure performance that results in the organization achieving its goals. A control system should encourage goal-oriented behavior. If the control system is too strong, behavior may be focused on the system and not on the objective.

A control system should provide a means for accomplishing the goals and not be an end in itself. Results are more important than standards. A well-designed control system can lead to management over control. The timing of receiving control information has to be determined. Certain performance factors need to be compared with standards every day, but much comparison is meaningful only after a period of time has elapsed.

The cost of controlling performance factors must also be considered and compared with the benefits. Relevant costs include direct financial costs and indirect costs, such as lost time and negative employee attitudes. The potential benefits can include resource conservation, timesaving, and quality improvements.

There is a general consensus that an effective control system should have some of the following characteristics:

1.   A control system should support the strategic plan.
2.   Significant issues need to be defined and measured. Those issues must impact the goals and objectives defined in the strategic plan.
3.   Information gathered should offer insights on deviations and why they occurred.
4.   It should be direct and simple.
5.   The system should be one which allows for the quick reporting of deviations in order that trends may be developed so corrections can occur before a problem becomes too big.
6.   Information should be concise and in understandable language.
7.   A good control system should allow those who make decisions to make them by complimenting the hierarchical structure.
8.   As in the Wal-Mart example, a good control system should provide for self-control whenever possible. Having people who have the ability to exercise self-control in the work place benefits the organization.
9.   Positive in nature, control systems ensure the success of the system by developing and nurturing change and improvements in the system.
10. Control systems should be impartial and separate from biased information.

Ethics and Control

Because of the intrusive nature of monitoring and controlling, there is an apparent conflict between an individual's right to privacy and a company's right to know. Companies claim that in order to meet their goals in today's highly competitive environment, they need to have workers who work efficiently. This not only means that they are willing to perform the tasks which they are assigned, but that they work in a safe manner. To do this they must perform their duties in a prescribed manner. Therefore, the company argues that monitoring is important to assure safe work habits.

Workers respond to this argument by saying that the company is only interested in profits and that if equipment, processes, and procedures are designed with safety in mind first and profits second, then intrusive monitoring would not be necessary.

Companies often counter, agreeing that they are in search of profits, but that this in itself is a motivator for safe operations since injured workers have a large negative impact on profits. Not only does the company lose a valued employee, but also its insurance rates can get prohibitively high.

Drug testing is another area with ethical implications. Some companies have resorted to voluntary and involuntary drug testing. This is done both before and during employment. The idea is to weed out those individuals who exhibit an inability to complete tasks due to foreign substance abuse. It is estimated that drug use in American plants costs U.S. organizations $100 billion a year. What this means is that costs increase at an alarming rate. Funds, which could be spent on community affairs and problems, are being spent in insurance claims and hospital bills instead, because of accidents.

In today's high-tech, fast paced, and highly competitive environment, companies are often competing with proprietary products and processes. Companies argue that keeping their information secret is a way of doing business and that they must make sure that no worker is passing this information on to competing companies.

Another area of contention is union sabotage. Workers sometimes, in a misguided attempt to support contract negotiators, have been known to slow down or report in sick. This is such a common occurrence that when police do this it has come to be known as the "blue flu." Some workers have been caught actually sabotaging equipment. Fortunately this is not too common.

All of these issues have become so important that developing good relations with workers and unions has become a way of achieving a competitive advantage. Remember the HRM area of your palette?

Summary

Just as a painter can not paint with his or her eyes closed, companies will find it difficult to be competitive without monitoring and controlling their operations. Monitoring and controlling is the last step in the strategic planning process. It closes the loop in the planning process providing valuable information, and allows you to constantly adjust your approach.

The control formula states that the need for action equals desired performance less actual performance (NFA = DP − AP). When actual performance is less than desired performance, there is a need for action. To implement this formula we looked at where to control and how to control.

The most important areas of concern when controlling should include (1) areas with a high potential for problems and (2) critical success areas. Organizations should also be concerned with over controlling, as this can often be just as problematic as under controlling.

The control process helps us implement this last step in the strategic planning process. The control process includes the following six steps:

1)   Determine what to control.
2)   Set control standards.
3)   Measure performance.
4)   Compare performance to standards.
5)   Determine reasons for deviations.
6)   Take corrective actions.

A good control system has ten attributes that facilitate the above six steps.

Finally, there are ethical considerations that must be considered when monitoring and controlling. Issues of conflict often occur around safety, drug testing, secrecy, and union activities. A competitive advantage can occur when these issues are resolved in a positive manner.

Conclusions

This book is about how you, as a person interested in getting into business, or you, the veteran business executive, can help lead your organization to long-term success and viability. Although there are many consultants and textbooks out there that say they can show you the way to success, none allows you to put into play your company's most valuable asset: you and your workforce's creativity.

To use your creativity we first developed a "strategic palette" which contained the source for every possible strategy and/or problem solution. We then utilized the strategic planning process to take our "paints" and create new and unique strategies. We looked at developing mission statements, setting goals and objectives, environmental scanning, financial tools, experience curves and product life cycles, portfolio modeling, implementation and finally monitoring and controlling. Now it is up to you. Remember, using the process from this book is not a guarantee of anything, but it sure can increase the probability of developing successful strategies and solutions for your organization. In today's dynamic and exciting environment, you need some luck and the ability to think creatively. Some people today call it "thinking outside the box."

With the advent of the internet and e-business there has never been a better time for a single person, using his or her own creative genius, which lives somewhere within all of us, to have such a dramatic impact. Good luck and remember **Paint to Win!**

Selected Sources

Alexander, Larry D., "Successfully Implementing Strategic Decisions", *Long Range Planning*: 1985. (18:3), pp. 91-97.

Arnold, Danny R.; Bizzel, Bobby G.; and Smith, Gary D., *Business Strategy and Policy*, 2nd ed., Houghton Mifflin Co.: Boston, 1988. 6: p.231-236 8: p. 227 9: p.232 10: p.233 11: p.254 12: p.235 13: p.236 14: p.237.

Bates, D.L., and Eldridge, David L., *Strategy and Policy: Analysis, Formulation, and Implementation*, Dubuque, Iowa: Wm. C. Brown Publishers. 1984.

Bowersox, Donald J, Staudt, Thomas A., Taylor, Donald A., *A Managerial Introduction to Marketing*; Prentice Hall; 1976.

Brandt, Steven C., *Strategic Planning in Emerging Companies:* Addison-Wesley Publishing Company; 1981.

Camillus, John C., *Strategic Planning and Management Control*, Lexington, Mass./Toronto: Lexington Books, D.C. Health and Co.: 1986.

Certo, Samuel C., and J. Paul Peter. *Strategic Management Concepts and Applications.* New York: Random House: 1988.

Chow, Irene; Hobert, Neil; Lone, Kelley; Yo, Julie, *Business Strategy*, Englewood Cliffe, NJ; Prentice Hall Inc.: 1997.

David, Bernard J., *Milestone Planning For Successful Ventures*, Boyd & Fraser Publishing Company: 1994.

David, Fred R. *Strategic Management*, 4e, New York: McMillan Publishing Co: 1993.

Digman, Lester A., *Strategic Management: Concepts, Decisions, Cases*, Plano, Texas: Business Publications Inc.: 1986.

Fahey, Liam, *The Strategic Management Reader*, Englewoods Cliffs, NJ, Prentice Hall, Inc.: 1989.

Fallon, William K., *AMA Management Handbook*. Amacom: New York: 1983. 16: p. 195 19: p. 202.

Finley, Lawrence, *Entrepreneurial Strategies*, PWS-Dent Publishing Company: 1990.

Flood, Patrick; Dromgoole, Tony; Carroll, Stephen J.; Gorman, Liam, *Managing Strategy implementation*, Blackwell Publishing: 2000.

Freeman, Edward R. *Strategic Management: A Stakeholder's Approach*, Marshfield, Mass.: University of Minnesota, Pitman Publishing Inc: 1984.

Gomez-Mejia, Luis R.; and Balkin, David B., *Compensation, Organizational Strategy, and Firm Performance*, Southwestern Publishing Co.: 1992.

Grant, Robert M., *Contemporary Strategy Analysis*, Third Edition, Blackwell Publishers: 1998.

Guth, Wm. D., and Macmillan, Ian C., "Strategy Implementation versus Middle Management Self Interest", *Strategic Management Journal*, (7:x), pp. 313-327. 1986.

Hayes, Robert, and Wheelwright, Steven, "Link Manufacturing Process and Product Life Cycles"; *Harvard Business Review*; 1976.

Hellriegel, Don and Slocum, John, *Management* 6th ed., Addison-Wesley: Boston: 1992. 2: p.618 3: p.617 4: p.619-620 7: p.619: p.626 17: p.636 18: p.301 21: p.637 22: p. 638.

Higgins, James M., and Vince, Julian W., *Strategic Management, Text and Cases*, 4th ed., The Dryden Press: Chicago: 1989. 5: p. 282-290 15: p. 291.

Hill, Charles and Gareth Jones, *Strategic Management: An Integrated Approach*, Boston: Houghton Mifflin: 1992.

Hofer, Charles W. & Schendel, Dan. *Strategy Formulation: Analytical Concepts*; West Publishing Company: 1982.

Hunger, David J. and Wheelen, Thomas L., *Strategic Management and Business Policy*, 8e, New York: Addison-Wesley Publishing Company, Inc.: 2002.

Hussey, D.E., "Implementing Corporate Strategy: Using Management Education and Training", *Long Range Planning*, 1985. (18:5), pp. 28-37.

Jouch, Lawrence R., and Glueck, Willeam F., *Business Policy and Strategic Management*, McGraw-Hill Book Company: 1988.

Kefalas, A.G., *Global Business Strategy*, Southwestern Publishing Co., Cincinnati, Ohio: 1990.

Kenny, Brian; Lea, Edward; Luffman, George; Sanderson, Stuart, *Business Policy: An Analytical Introduction*; Basil Blackwell Ltd.: 1991.

Kuhn, Robert L., *Creativity and Strategy in Mid-Sized Firms*, Inglewoods Cliffs, NJ, Prentice Hall Inc.: 1989.

Linstone, Harold A., *Multiple Perspectives For Decision Making, Bridging the Gap Between Analysis and Action*, New York: Elsevier Science Publishing Co.: 1984.

Michaels, Ronald; Olshavsky, Richard; Qualls, William. "Shortening of the PLC - an Empirical Test", *Journal of Marketing*; 1981.

Montanari: Morgan; and Brocker, *Strategic Management a Choice Approach*, Dryden Press: 1990.

Mumford, Enid and Andrew Pettigrew, *Implementing Strategic Decisions*, London: Longman: 1975.

Nutt, Paul C., "Implementing Approaches for Project Planning", *Academy of Management Review*: 1983. (8:4), pp. 600-611.

Osteryoung, Jerome S., and Denslow, Diane L., *So You Need To Write A Business Plan*, South-Western: 2003.

Pearce II, John A. and Richard B. Robinson, Jr., *Strategic Management: Strategy Formulation and Implementation*, 3e, Homewood, Illinois: Richard D. Irwin, Inc.: 1988.

Porter, M. E., *Competitive Strategy,* Free Press: 1980.

Porter, M. E., *Competitive Advantage,* Free Press: 1985.

Prusad, Benjamin S., *Policy, Strategy, and Implementation: Text and Cases with a Global View*, New York: Random House: 1983.

Reed, Richard and Buckley, Ronald M., "Strategy in Action-Techniques for Implementing Strategy", *Long Range Planning*: 1988. (21:3) 1, pp. 67-74.

Ries, Al; Trout, Jack, *Marketing Warfare*, New York, McGraw-Hill: 1986.

Rink, David R. and Swan, John E., "Product Life Cycle Research: A Literature Review", Journal of Business Research; Sept. 1979.

Saloner, G.; Shepard, Andrea; Podolny, Joel, *Strategic Management*, John Wiley & Sons: 2001.

Schermerhorn, John R., *Management for Productivity*, Wiley and Sons: New York: 1992. 20: p. 418.

Sharplin, Arthur, *Strategic Management*, USA: McGraw-Hill, Inc.: 1985.

Smith, Gary D. Arnold, Danny R., Biell, Bobby G., *Business Strategy and Policy*, 2nd ed., Boston: Houghton Mifflin Co.: 1988.

Thompson, A., Strickland, A.S., *Strategic Management: An Integrated Approach*, Boston: Houghton Mifflin: 1992.

Weiss, Alan, *Making It Work*, New York: Harper Business: 1990.

Wernham, Roy, "Bridging the Awful Gap Between Strategy and Action", *Long Range Planning*, 1984. (17:6), pp. 34-42.

Willis, Raymond E., *A Guide to Forecasting for Planners and Managers*, Englewood Cliffs, NJ: Prentice-Hall, Inc.: 1987.

Wright, Peter; Kroll, Mark J.; Parnell, John; *Strategic Management Concepts and Cases*, 3e, Prentice Hall: 1996.

Yoffie, David B., *Strategic Management In Information Technology*, Prentice Hall: 1994.